HARNESSING GLOBAL POTENTIAL

10650323

POTENTIAL

INSIGHTS INTO MANAGING CUSTOMERS WORLDWIDE

Kevin Wilson, Tony Millman, Dan Weilbaker
and Simon Croom

Harnessing Global Potential

Insights into Managing Customers Worldwide

Edited By:

Lisa Napolitano
Executive Director, SAMA

Contributing Authors:

Dr. Kevin Wilson
CEO, Sales Research Trust Ltd., U.K.

Tony Millman
Professor of Int'l Business & Mktg., University of Buckingham, U.K.

Dr. Dan C. Weilbaker
Standard Register Professor of Sales, Northern Illinois University, U.S.

Dr. Simon Croom
Lecturer in Operations Management, Warwick Business School, U.K.

Copyright © 2001 – Strategic Account Management Association

All rights reserved.

For information about permission to reproduce selections from this book, write to:

Permissions, Strategic Account Management Association
150 N. Wacker Drive, Suite 2222, Chicago, IL 60606
Tel: 312-251-3131   Fax: 312-251-3132
Internet: www.strategicaccounts.org

Library of Congress Cataloging-in-Publication Data

Harnessing Global Potential: Insights into Managing Customer Worldwide / Kevin Wilson, Tony Millman, Dan Weilbaker, Simon Croom

ISBN 0-9657422-8-8 $19.95

Printed in the United States of America.

Table of Contents

INTRODUCTION

Defining the Challenge

INTRODUCTION

Definition: A *Global Account* is one that has strategic importance to the achievement of the supplier's corporate objectives, pursues integrated and coordinated strategies on a worldwide basis, and demands a globally integrated product/service from its suppliers.

Global Account Management (GAM) is a selling company's response to the challenge of managing strategically important customers who are facing increasing globalization of their industries. As these customers extend their global reach and intensify their foreign investment, they seek greater coordination and integration of their activities worldwide, and they invariably turn to their existing suppliers to make similar commitments in order to ensure consistent service/support. No matter whether GAM is buyer or seller-initiated, both parties soon recognize their interdependence and the urgent need to address the so-called "global/local" dilemma, i.e., the question of how global and how local their approach should be in particular industries.

> *Our strategy is built around customers and is based on three principles. We must have excellence in execution; we must offer global consistency; and we must deliver local expertise.*
>
> *Robert Binney, Citibank*

Our concept of GAM strategy is firmly embedded in the broader fields of global, corporate, business, and marketing strategy, with due consideration given to global supply chains/networks and commercial/industrial settings. To this end, two interrelated tenets of GAM have served us well:

- Maintain a holistic view of global operations without losing sight of the needs of far-flung parts
- Centralize those activities that are best managed and coordinated centrally, and decentralize other activities to the people close to customers/markets so as to enhance local knowledge and responsiveness

Given these tenets, it is relatively easy to see how the notion of *global* account management might begin to fit with *regional* and *national* account/sales management. Although this book focuses predominantly on the global level of aggregation, we are very aware of the kind of organizational and cultural issues that arise at regional and national levels, and how these issues can stifle global initiatives. When rolling out a GAM program, exhortations to coordinate and integrate operations across borders become meaningless without buy-in at all three levels.

When discussing GAM, National Account Management (NAM) is important because it is where most of our cumulative learning and experience resides. Reliance upon a national geographical model of account management is less tenable in a world where trade spills over national borders and where there is greater global interdependence among companies, subsidiaries, and countries. While it may have served semiautonomous multinational customer operations well, it has less relevance when organizations are battling with the complexity of coordinating the supply of multiple products and services to/from multiple locations, building multiple levels of customer contact across national borders, encouraging cross-selling, and so on. These developments have far-reaching implications for devising global/local strategies and for implementing appropriate structures, systems, and processes.

Our challenge in writing this book has been to capture the dynamics of globalization and to present a coherent response in the form of an approach to GAM. In reality, we have provided no more than a partial response—a work in progress—mainly because GAM is still in its infancy and many selling companies continue to experiment with their programs.

The source of our material is twofold: we have drawn from our collective experiences as researchers and consultants in the field of strategic account management over many years, and we refer extensively to findings from our recent study of GAM practices in U.S. and European companies. This study was conducted by The Sales Research Trust (SRT) and sponsored by the Strategic Account Management Association (SAMA). In this respect, we did not set out to produce a report for academic consumption, though we applied academic rigor nevertheless. Our mission is to inform rather than to impress. Our book should, therefore, be judged primarily against the twin criteria of readability and managerial relevance.

The structure of the book is organized around a number of interrelated themes that will be explored using the insights we have gained from our own research and the limited work that has been done by other colleagues in the field. In order to illustrate these themes, we will refer to a wide range of managerial experience provided by the senior executives and global account managers who have wrestled with challenges and have developed solutions that work for them.

Eight broad themes are explored in the following chapters. First we explore the nature of the *Global Business Environment*, the drivers and the impact of globalization upon individual industries. The degree of globalization varies from industry to industry as well as from company to company. It is therefore important to align global account management strategies to the level of globalization apparent in the industry and the global capabilities of both the company and their customers.

Next we discuss *Buyer-Supplier Responses to Globalization*. We stress the importance of context and argue that the strategic options open to supplier organizations are constrained by both their own and the customer's global capabilities, strategic focus, and relational culture.

Under the heading *Getting Started*, we examine several issues that need to be addressed to ensure a smooth transition from NAM to GAM, such as senior executive engagement, managerial and team appointments, the selection of global accounts, and the development of supporting organizational structures, systems, and processes. Where possible, we have sought practitioner advice (presented in the form of vignettes and short quotations) to reinforce our message about the necessity for thorough up-front preparation and a systematic approach. Not surprisingly, this is a pivotal section in our exposition of GAM practice.

We then explore how companies have set about *Building the Competencies* in terms of the underpinning structures, systems, and processes that support the GAM program. This chapter draws heavily upon managerial experience and provides a number of miniature case studies that afford insights into the approaches adopted by specific companies. It is apparent that GAM programs disrupt established practice and threaten entrenched perceptions and positions, and we address the question of culture, from both a national and an organizational viewpoint, and the approaches companies have adopted to overcome the organizational barriers to GAM implementation.

Returning to our earlier theme that GAM should not exist in isolation, the next section takes the perspective of the strategic account relationship as merely one component in an overall *Global Supply Chain*. Industry and company initiatives in the area of supply chain integration/optimization, for example, are demanding greater transparency of the cost and value accumulation process, and there is growing interest in the notion of competing supply chains.

The nature of the role performed by the *Global Account Manager* is critical to the success of GAM programs. We explore his/her mediating role at two critical interfaces: first, the *internal* interfaces, such as those between the supplier's headquarters and business units, or between business units; and second, the many *external* interfaces among headquarters and dispersed business units of both the supplier and customer. This leads us logically to assess the set of skills/competencies required to perform the role of Global Account Manager and one particular subset of metaskills/competencies related to what has been called the role of *political entrepreneur*.

Under the heading *Managing the Process*, we paint a broad picture of organizational complexity and cultural diversity, representing the backdrop against which GAM programs must be implemented. Drawing heavily on practitioner experience, we cover a range of factors impinging upon the process of implementation and extract a few guidelines for best practice.

And finally, building on and learning from past experience, we pull together a few thoughts on critical developments and speculate about the *Future Direction of GAM*. In

GAM we are seeing the emergence of a new managerial process that will have an enormous impact, not merely upon buyer/seller relationships, but upon the very fabric of international business and economic organization.

"The question for all companies, in all industries and all around the world, is not _whether_ to go global. The question is _when?_ The truth is that, as your customers increasingly globalize their operations, you must be able to serve them consistently wherever they operate in the world or you will soon cease to serve them _anywhere_ in the world."

CHAPTER I

The Global Business Environment

CHAPTER I: THE GLOBAL BUSINESS ENVIRONMENT

In this chapter we:

- **Take a holistic view of the global business environment**
- **Identify some of the key drivers of globalization**
- **Allude to developments in several globalizing industries**
- **Review the impact of globalization**

Introduction

One of the most well known "open systems" approaches to strategic management is to consider the internal organizational response of companies to changes in their external business environment. This is not to suggest that companies should be permanently in response mode, or that they should merely adapt their offerings and organizational structures/systems to changes in customer requirements and competitive behavior. An effective strategic response is typically a blend of reactive and proactive behavior predicated upon a thorough understanding of the dynamics of the business environment, giving due regard to the underlying driving forces for both change and stability.

We subscribe heavily to the old adage that companies should strive to become "customer focused and market driven." One of the dangers lurking in strategic account management is overemphasis on the former to the relative neglect of the latter. The simple message here is that customers operate in markets and industries, and different markets/industries are globalizing at different rates. Without some sense of this globalization process and its impact on customers, it is impossible to assess some of the major determinants of strategic account attractiveness, such as growth potential and political/financial risk.

We will now turn our attention to characterizing the main drivers of globalization in business-to-business markets.

Drivers of Globalization

Growing Worldwide Competition
During the latter half of the twentieth century we saw a number of developments that increased the intensity of competition in world markets. First, the return of Japan, Germany, and other European countries to challenge for leading positions in world trade; secondly, the formation of the European Union to rival the political and economic power of North America; and third, the growth of multinational companies as a channel for trade and investment. This predominantly Western capitalist perspective on growth and competition was not a smooth progression: there were protracted wars in Korea and Vietnam, sporadic military conflicts in other parts of the world, and three oil shocks to contend with—all providing major distractions and dislocations.

Discussions relating to economic growth and competition in the "free world" tended to ignore what was happening in the Soviet Union, Eastern/Central Europe, and Asia, apart from perhaps the phenomenal growth of Japan and the tiger economies and occasional references to the "promise" of China and India. In particular, the collapse of the Soviet

Union and the end of the Cold War in 1989 wreaked havoc among its trading bloc partners, many of whom have since declared their future to lie with an enlarged European Union. These developments open up markets previously inaccessible and bring new competitors who threaten the status quo, but their impact will pale into insignificance compared with the entry of highly populated and low labor cost countries such as China and India into the world trading system.

Structural Changes in Many Industries
Three broad structural changes can be discerned in many economies around the world that appear to be driving globalization:

- Deregulation of government owned or sanctioned utility monopolies
- Mergers and acquisitions resulting in consolidation
- Simultaneous development of centers of technological innovation in multiple worldwide locations

Deregulation: Deregulation of government-sanctioned monopolies frees up competition and, in the case of government owned monopolies, is often accompanied by full or part privatization and relaxation of restrictions on foreign direct investment. Some countries (e.g., the U.S. and the U.K.) are well advanced along this path towards a more open economy. Others are at various stages of deregulation and are finding it a painful process of adjustment (e.g., France, Germany, and most notably the economies linked to the former Soviet Union). Powerful nations call the shots at the global level, and at the national level, governments appoint regulatory bodies or "watchdogs" and introduce licensing procedures. Most countries also attempt to protect their "flag carriers" as though they symbolize national virility!

Many of these deregulated organizations are in the forefront of the globalization phenomenon. In telecommunications, we look to the example of British Telecom, and in the field of logistics, Deutsche Post, both of which are rapidly becoming global players through merger and acquisition following deregulation.

Mergers and Acquisitions: Recent mergers and acquisitions, together with a plethora of strategic alliances, are changing the structure of industries and markets. Increasing consolidation is occurring in many industries between international companies. The effect is the creation of organizations that span the globe and, as a result, attempt to coordinate and integrate their worldwide operations. This is true both of companies operating in broad markets and of those operating in specialized niches.

This has a ripple effect on supply chains and may radically change account relationships. For example, customers who were once regarded as separate discrete entities in a neat portfolio of strategic accounts now find themselves merged into a bigger and more complex entity—part of the new entity may have long been a loyal customer and another part may have been a competitor's customer. What follows is a period of instability and accommodation, during which the enlarged customer looks for cost savings and suppliers compete for what they think is their rightful share of the combined business. New owners and incoming managers may have different priorities regarding partnership and the supply relationship may take several months to settle down into some semblance of order.

In most industries, globalization forces rationalization of

supply bases, resulting in the formation of first, second and lower tiers of suppliers, who themselves consolidate to survive and preserve their status. Motor vehicles, aerospace, food, and electronics provide examples. Some industries, notably retailing, remained at a relatively slow pace of globalization for many years with expansion taking place primarily on a national or regional basis. Then, suddenly, globalization was triggered by the strategic moves of one major player and what seemed an orderly and predictable market became highly uncertain. Such was the case in retailing, for example, when the world's largest retailer, Wal-Mart, made acquisitions in Germany and the U.K. This had reverberations throughout supply chains and has changed the face of retailing in Europe.

The Structure of Technological Innovation: Historically, the locus of technological innovation has generally been geographically focused, if transient. For example, the first industrial revolution originated in the United Kingdom with subsequent waves of innovation emanating first from Germany and then from the United States. Early technological advances were concerned with *hard technologies* (e.g., steel, combustion engines, jet propulsion, communication equipment, computer development) followed by a focus on innovation to processes, i.e., *soft technologies.* For example, in the 1980s, Japan and the Pacific Rim provided the center for improvements to business processes that fuelled the rise of Japan to world economic dominance.

The most recent wave of technological change has been concerned with knowledge-based technology and has been structural in nature. Whereas technological initiatives were predominately focused around individual centers of operation, there is now a tendency for such initiatives to be occurring around the world in parallel. For example, Silicon

Valley can no longer claim a near monopoly on software development, but must share the claim with Northern India. In addition, information technologies are being simultaneously developed in Finland, the U.S., and Japan. Companies that want to keep abreast of innovation need to have a presence wherever technological developments are occurring.

Saturation of Domestic Markets

From a Western perspective it has become increasingly difficult to maintain double-digit top-line growth in home markets. Given the maturity of many product markets in North America and Western Europe, multinational companies have been forced to look elsewhere. Apart from attacking each other's domestic markets, both American and European companies have targeted Asia and South America as the main regions for increasing sales of products/services, which range from basic infrastructure projects to fast-moving consumer goods and financial services.

This driving need to sustain historical levels of growth presents a serious challenge for multinational companies. That there is latent demand for their products/services is seldom a contentious issue. The challenge lies in their ability to cope with organizational complexity and cultural diversity as they extend their reach into geographical regions of which they have little working knowledge of customer behavior and ways of doing business. Our experience suggests that if U.S. and European multinationals attempt to force their predominantly Western management practices on their foreign subsidiaries and strategic accounts, then penetration will be frustratingly slow and disappointing. These "high context" cultures require a much more sensitive and flexible approach than multinationals have applied hitherto.

Convergence of Information / Communication Technology

The long-awaited convergence of computer hardware/software technologies with telecommunications technologies is now being delivered. Not perhaps with the much-hyped promise of the "paperless office" and the "factory of the future" of two decades ago, but employing a more realistic and pragmatic approach with vendors who are more attuned to the human aspects of implementation.

Telephone, fax, and teleconferencing provide obvious examples of information/communication network connectivity that has greatly enhanced the operations of multinational companies. More recently, video conferencing, e-mail, web conferencing, and the use of sophisticated corporate Extranets and Intranets have transformed information-intensive operations underpinning a wide range of manufacturing and service industries.

Computer databases and associated applications software, for example, are now a "given" for participation in airline alliance networks, financial services, and the secretive world of military command/control systems. In manufacturing industries, converging technologies have enhanced the possibilities for greater cross-border integration of design, production, and logistics, enabling some companies to span time zones by "following the sunrise."

Transferability of Corporate Brand Image

Generally speaking, the greater the transferability of corporate brand image worldwide, the easier it is to develop global value propositions and increase global reach. This transfer is, of course, greatly enhanced by a high degree of standardization of product/service offerings. This is particularly noticeable where there are opportunities to exploit similar consumer purchasing preferences and pursue global/regional communications strategies. In contrast, in industrial and business-to-business markets where corporate brands tend to be less in the public eye, their impact is nonetheless important because reputation is critical in establishing credibility and global presence.

The Implications of Globalization

First and foremost, it must be pointed out that the implications of globalization for companies are uneven. While it may be fashionable to talk of increasing homogeneity and interconnectivity, compression of time and space, etc., there are countervailing trends in the business environment at a regional and national level that shape account management strategies.

> ★ Multinational companies, by definition, have a history of restricting their operations to a set of relatively autonomous countries. Globalization and regionalization of their business environment exposes them to other business models and cultures, and requires much greater attention to the forces driving cross-border coordination and integration.

No economy can realistically regard itself as immune from the forces of globalization, but let us not forget the enduring geopolitical concept of the "nation-state" and how it interprets itself in a world characterized by vastly differing degrees of economic development and political/religious ideologies. In short, developments in some parts of the world and in some industries are just not possible at the rate and magnitude experienced so far in Europe and North America.

Nevertheless, the fact that globalization is occurring at an accelerated rate means that companies, regardless of size, are faced with addressing globalization issues. The sooner a company faces these challenges the better prepared they will be for survival.

CHAPTER II

Buyer-Supplier Responses To Globalization

CHAPTER II: BUYER-SUPPLIER RESPONSES TO GLOBALIZATION

In this chapter we:

- Take a holistic view of the global business environment
- Explore organizational responses to globalization
- Discuss the characteristics of global companies
- Identify the differences between national, international, regional and global companies
- Understand why these differences are important
- Identify the organizational prerequisites of GAM programs

Introduction

Chapter One explored the impact of globalization at the industry level: the increasing consolidation of industries with fewer, but much larger, players; the commoditization of even the most technologically rich products; and the increasing competitive pressure to compress cost, time, and space. This chapter considers the response at the organizational level to the drivers of globalization.

Access To New Markets

One obvious response to the slowdown of growth in domestic markets is the increase in the organization's international operations in order to access new markets. This may simply involve the establishment of trading relationships that facilitate the export of "home grown" products, or it may extend to the establishment of sales and marketing operations, warehousing facilities, or the manufacture of product under license. The firm may ultimately establish partnerships or wholly owned subsidiary operations, which source, manufacture, and market all over the world. As firms increase their global reach, they also begin to source globally and/or expect their *national* suppliers to go global with them.

Customers are demanding a uniform product/service offering, the same delivery schedules, the same level of support services, and the same pricing structures from their suppliers—wherever they operate in the world. The major response by sellers has been the attempt to develop GAM programs in order to meet the demands of their most strategically important customers.

Global Agreements Drive Down Costs

A primary motivation for customers in offering global agreements to their suppliers has been the desire to drive

The benefits of global agreements to the customer? They see only one and that's cost. That's their deal.
Ed Bollman, Bussman Corporation

down cost. Increasing internationalization is seen as a way of achieving economies of scale through lower prices, product standardization, process economies, inventory management, and the refinement of logistical capabilities. In the early stages of global buyer-supplier relationships there is a tendency for customers to focus upon the opportunity to negotiate global pricing agreements. It may come as no surprise that if they are paying $1.50 in the U.S.,

$1.00 in Europe and 75 cents in Asia, then the *global* price they want to negotiate is 75 cents. There is, however, a growing recognition by customers that the competencies of their suppliers can be instrumental in helping them to create differential advantage in their own markets. The initial motivation may still be primarily focused upon cost reduction through supplier reduction programs, supply chain management initiatives and buyer-supplier partnership arrangements, but as global relationships mature there comes a recognition that supplier capabilities may be harnessed to achieve far more than just cost reduction.

> One of the factors is that going global actually reduces logistics costs. If world markets are prepared to accept a standardized product and you manufacture around the world you save on the cost of raw materials because of your purchasing power and you save on logistics because you are manufacturing close to the market.
>
> Paul Crunkleton, Eastman Chemical

Early GAM Programs Tend To Be Reactive

Seller initiatives to establish GAM programs are primarily a response to customer demand and represent an attempt to create competitive differentiation through achieving economies in operations or logistics and to enhance the level of service provided to their key global customers. In essence these initiatives are fundamentally reactive. They reflect a realization that if they do not provide an integrated global offering, then their competitors will and not only will they loose out on global business, they will in all probability loose the local business as well.

As suppliers' experience of operating globally grows, so they begin to recognize that there are major opportunities

In our case it was customer driven. We had a customer a few years back and they said, "We're going into Canada". We said "Great, we have an agent up there". They said, "No, you don't understand. We're going to Canada and you're going to be there, not with an agent, but as Fritz." So we had to go out and acquire a company in Canada. Some of our major customers took us (global), in some cases kicking and screaming. So I can honestly say it's like the 800lb gorilla—you go anywhere he says.

John Fitzgerald, Fritz Companies

to work with customers, not only to defend their own business but also to enhance the total value created for both buyer and seller within the relationship. Going global represents an opportunity to develop and refine competencies that have broader application than cost reduction, product standardization or logistical integration.

The drivers of globalization have had a fundamental impact upon business processes, the demands that buyers and sellers place upon each other and upon the nature of the interaction between them.

Being An International Company Doesn't Make You A Global Company

In responding to the stimulus of globalization both customers and their suppliers have been required to make major changes to organizational structures, systems and processes. In many cases they have also been required to change the culture within the organization in that there is often a fundamental need to recognize that being a *global company* is not the same as being an *international company*.

> *Initially the driver is pricing, but what its really about is recognizing the customer as a global entity and recognizing their varying needs in their different locations, the organizational complexity and the strategic imperatives.*
>
> *Dave Potter, Xerox*

Two fundamental questions are:

1. What is a global company?
2. Why is it important to know?

Many companies take a pragmatic approach to defining global accounts or differentiating between different types of strategic accounts. On the other hand, some notable companies, Hewlett Packard for example, have moved beyond using classifications based upon geographical spread to identify global customers.

> *Customers have been able to become global because they are flexible and responsive and in part they get that from their suppliers. They are easy to do business with but they demand creative, responsive, and varied selling methods and solutions.*
>
> *Tom McCarty, Motorola*

In the first case, where the term is used loosely to describe virtually any strategic customer that operates internationally, this tends to reflect a relatively unsophisticated approach on the part of the supplier to the management of their strategic accounts across the world. They tend to recognize only the potential the customer represents for increased business rather than some of the fundamental differences that exist between *national, international, regional,* and truly *global* customers.

In the case of more experienced suppliers they do recognize the important differences between the operating characteristics of their global customers and others that adopt different forms of international organization. This knowledge is embedded in the supplier organization, as is the knowledge that some international or regional customers may be of equal, or greater importance than *global* ones. This knowledge is reflected in the different approaches that the supplier adopts to serve different types of customers.

★ One example given was of a Japanese company that was treated by its U.S. supplier as a global account despite the fact that they had no operating plants outside Japan. They had such a dominant technological position in their industry that they had to be treated like a global account in the opinion of their supplier.

In our view, the question of what is, or is not, a *global customer* or a *global supplier* is an important one. As one of the respondents to our research suggested: "If you have a global agreement with a nonglobal company, you don't have a global agreement, you have a hunting license." The term *global* is, in practice, problematic. Often, when talking to suppliers, we found only a loose understanding of what they mean by a *global customer.* Some suppliers identified any major customer operating *internationally* as a *global* account, while for others, any account that is of strategic importance, whether or not they have widespread international operations.

As we suggested in the previous chapter, the level of globalization in any particular industry will vary. Nevertheless, in most industries, many of your strategically important customers are operating in many parts of the world

We're probably one of those companies that think we're in some sort of global program and now we're just starting to realize that we're not. One of the problems is that our customers are not really global—they are really international companies. We probably do not differentiate. The way we are structured here, as far as handling accounts is concerned, is that if it is in multi-country locations, then it is simply a global account. If it is in Mexico or Canada, then we consider them just like a North American account, but once we cross salt water then we start throwing definitions at them, whatever those definitions may be. The other problem is with us. In Europe we have a general manager who is responsible for everything over there, three manufacturing units in the U.K., one in Denmark. He's also responsible for sales and marketing and is rewarded for throughput out of the facilities he's responsible for. That kills me when I go to the U.K. and say we need to sell more North American product in Europe. They say, 'we agree 100% but our boss isn't rewarded for selling your product.'

Respondent to the GAM Research Study

and are demanding what *they* perceive as a global offering from their suppliers. They want a uniform product offering, the same delivery schedules, the same level of service support and they also want a uniform pricing structure, wherever it is that they are doing business, and whether or not they are structured *globally*. This is probably the single most important driver of the development of GAM programs and the reason why, even though they may be viewed as an extension of *national* account management programs, they may need to be approached differently.

So What Is A Global Company?
The definition that we gave of a *global account* in the Introduction provides some clues as to what we define as a

global company. There, we said that "A *global* account is one that is of strategic importance to the achievement of the supplier's corporate objectives, pursues integrated and coordinated strategies on a worldwide basis and demands a globally integrated product/service offering from its suppliers." We shall expand upon that definition in later chapters when we discuss Global Account selection but in helping us to define what we mean by a *global company* two elements of this statement are important. Firstly a global company operates internationally, not necessarily in all parts of the world but in a number of different regions (South East Asia, North America, Europe, etc.). Secondly, and possibly most importantly, they integrate and coordinate their operations wherever they operate worldwide.

It is rare that companies are able to move from being national players to being global players overnight. There tends to be a gradual increase in the internationalization of their operations as they mover from exporting, through developing international marketing and manufacturing capabilities, to the establishment of regional operations before they transition to being truly global players.

National companies tend to display high levels of centralization in decision-making and operations and, quite naturally, the country in which they operate shapes their cultural perspective. They will therefore adopt the business norms and practices of their own country and rely heavily upon other national companies to provide both their supplier and customer base. They may well use foreign suppliers and may take advantage of the lower cost associated with the offerings of global suppliers (standardized products etc), but are usually incapable of capitalizing upon the enhanced value potential that doing business with global suppliers may represent. Unless they have ownership of particular processes, technology, or markets that are par-

Figure 1: Different Types of Account Relationships

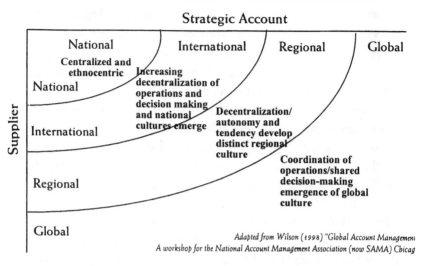

Adapted from Wilson (1998) "Global Account Management
A workshop for the National Account Management Association (now SAMA) Chicag

ticularly important to the global supplier, they are unlikely to be perceived as strategic accounts. Similarly, while they may well export, they have neither the geographical presence nor organizational capability to effectively serve the needs of international companies.

International companies are at a transitional stage and may display varying degrees of centralization and decentralization. Initially, foreign operations may be rigidly controlled from headquarters in the "home" territory, but as marketing, manufacturing, and procurement are increasingly devolved to "local" managers, so decision-making structures and operational control tend to become fragmented. In extreme cases, individual country facilities become operational silos, in effect independent units, which to some degree at least adopt the culture of the host country. In some respects, the international operator with multiple independent operational locations has similar problems in receiving or making *global* offerings to other national companies. Despite the fact that they may have wide geographical spread, they lack coordination and uniformity of decision-making. This makes operating collectively very difficult. Attempts to impose a unified strategic approach towards international markets or supply chains may be sabotaged by country managers who consider that their *local* fiscal and political interests may not be best served.

Regional companies are those that have operations in many different countries, which they have grouped together to reflect broader geographical boundaries. For example, a company may have operating plants and marketing operations in several European countries all of which come under the direct control of a European general manager. Here we may witness varying degrees of operational integration to serve Pan-European customers, to achieve economies of scale and scope or to better manage the supplier base. The degree to which these organizations perceive their regional operations to be integrated will influence the degree to which the organization adopts multicultural perspectives. There may still be a tendency for one culture to dominate depending upon the degree of centralized control exercised by the European or South East Asian or South American *headquarters*. Regional companies are usually well able to meet the needs of major national accounts in the various countries within each region. They may also be adept at meeting the needs of Regional Strategic Accounts but often lack the coordination and commonality of interest between regions that would allow them to serve Global customers or receive the full value of global offerings made by their suppliers.

It is possible to envisage sixteen different *theoretical* buyer-seller relationships from this model (e.g., global supplier/global customer; national supplier/global customer; global supplier/national customer; etc.) that have implications for the ways in which buyers and sellers interact in terms of:

- Decision-making processes
- Cultural diversity
- Organizational complexity
- Information management and exchange
- Logistical and operational coordination
- Approaches to pricing

All the sixteen relational states are possible, but in global terms, only a few have the potential for the creation of synergistic value beyond the exchange of goods and services. The demands of regional and global customers far outstrip the ability of national and international suppliers to effectively manage these elements of the interaction process.

Developing GAM programs is expensive in terms of hard cash, human resources, and time. The cost of getting it wrong can be even greater. A "sure fire" way of getting it wrong is to try to develop a global program when either you do not have the capability (i.e., you are a national or international company) or where your customers do not have the *global* capability to accept your global offering. In those cases, it is still essential to develop a SAM (*Strategic Account Management*) program for those customers, but it will not be *global* in nature.

Ultimately, suppliers must be clear about their own capability to deliver, and their customers' ability to receive a global offering.

★ Atul Parvatiyar and Thomas Gruen from Emory University have done some work in this area and they have identified three categories of global company. They suggest that whether a GAM program will achieve seller/customer goals is contingent upon the type of global account selected by the supplier, the global capability of the supplier and upon features of the GAM program. They suggest that companies can be classified as global players, global transitionals and global aspirant. Global Players are large geocentric organizations with worldwide integration of all major business functions. Global Transitionals are medium sized companies exhibiting some degree of central coordination and integration of worldwide. They may exhibit regiocentric of geocentric orientations and perceive a high need to develop global capabilities in order to align with global customers. Global Aspirants are generally ethnocentric companies in the early stages of global expansion. Only global players can serve the needs of a full range of customers and suppliers should therefore choose customers on the basis of their attractiveness, the ability of the supplier to serve them globally and the level of resource and expertise available.

Parvatiyar and Gruen, 1999, "A Contingency Model of Global Account Management" Working Paper presented at the 3rd International Symposium on Selling and Major Account Management, Southampton, U.K., July 1999.

Getting To The Starting Block

Three conclusions may be drawn from these observations: Firstly, in developing GAM programs companies should adopt a portfolio approach, segmenting their *international* customers on the basis of their degree of globalization as well as their level of strategic attractiveness. Secondly, in order to compete effectively in global markets they must develop the organizational capability to support their global aspirations and enable them to make differential of-

I want my (global) customers to look at my company and see us, not as a product supplier, but as a $12 billion service company with a significant investment in strategic core competencies that can be leveraged against issues that keep them awake at night.

ferings throughout their portfolio of customers. Finally, they must design *tailored* global value propositions for individual customers that go far beyond the provision of products with global applications.

Our research suggests that before embarking upon portfolio analysis or the development of global value propositions companies must address a number of key issues. These issues will be the subject of more detailed discussion as we develop the themes of *Getting Started, Building the Competencies,* and *Sustaining the Effort* in later sections of this book. For the moment it is useful to summarize those elements of the GAM program that need to be in place from the outset.

Senior Management Entanglement

Tacit support for the GAM process from senior management is not enough. GAM programs will have a major impact upon existing systems and processes and upon established political positions within the firm. If the radical changes that are required are to take effect, then senior managers must be *entangled* in the process, demonstrating its importance throughout the organization. In addition, middle management must also be convinced of the value the program and this requires that the needs of local management are integrated into the global strategy and communicated effectively to all management levels.

"It comes right from the top of our management team, from the Chairman to the President — and everyone is aware of it."

The Global Account Manager

Part of the process of Demonstrating senior management commitment is the positioning of the global account management role within the organization. The global account manager should have a direct access to senior managers and be seen to receive his/her remit directly from them.

Strong National Account Management Capabilities

Successful global suppliers have all exhibited strong capabilities in managing national accounts and this supports the idea that GAM extends the concept of national account management into areas of greater geographical scope and organizational/cultural complexity. What should be remembered, however, is that the scale of organizational complexity and cultural diversity and the difficulties of coordinating global operations and networks of contacts both within the supplier and customer organizations, makes GAM *qualitatively* different from NAM.

Coordinated Internal Systems, Structures, Processes

A fundamental requirement for companies wishing to serve their global customers is to coordinate their global operations. Those who embark successfully on GAM programs have already made significant effort to integrate global procurement, manufacturing and marketing processes. They have developed internal communications processes and configured their logistical processes to integrate effectively with their customer supply chains. Part of the process of realigning internal systems and processes is to address issues of reward and compensation to facilitate the local implementation of the global strategy. Companies who do not recognize the importance of this issue will perpetuate the local/global divide and it is extremely difficult to imple-

> *There is a tremendous need for global coordination. Right now it doesn't happen. Our VP manufacturing is only responsible for the five plants we have in the U.S.. We've got another nine facilities he has nothing to do with!*

ment GAM programs where local service providers see no value for themselves.

In addition, a common information system that acts as a platform for communications with customers and with supplier personnel around the world as well as facilitating the collection of data relating to the global relationship provides companies initiating GAM programs with considerable advantage.

> *Logistics is very important, as is international monetary capabilities and information technology. At the moment I would say that our global communications capabilities exceed what our customers can do and in a way, that knowledge is part of what we give away as part of the value we create.*

CHAPTER III

Getting Started: Initiating GAM Programs

Chapter III: Getting Started – Initiating GAM Programs

In this chapter we:

- Identify three factors required before embarking on GAM
- Stress selling a GAM program internally
- Examine the selection of global account managers
- Identify potential global accounts from a portfolio of candidates
- Discuss the importance of communication infrastructures
- Discuss the importance of the compensation program
- Discuss the importance of real time account planning and reporting
- Begin the transition from NAM to GAM

Introduction

In Chapter Two we examined organizational responses to globalization and discussed the nature of global operations. This chapter is divided into three sections that provide a sequential framework for starting a GAM program. **Section One** discusses the issues that are critical to have in place before attempting to develop a GAM program. **Section Two** identifies and discusses the issues that need to be developed once the pre-GAM factors are in place. Finally,

Section Three explores some of the factors that facilitate or hinder the implementation of GAM programs.

Section 1: Pre-GAM Organizational Requirements

Our GAM research suggests that there are a number of organizational prerequisites for the effective initiation of a GAM program. In order to launch a GAM program successfully, the supplier must be capable of delivering a product or service with global applications. However, that is just the price of entry for a GAM program. In addition to the global offering, suppliers also need to have an established and successful NAM program. If these two factors are in place then the supplier needs to have senior level sponsorship and be managed from near the strategic apex of the firm in order to ensure that there is the political will to drive the program through.

A Global Product / Service Delivery Capability
The effective support of GAM programs appears to be strongly dependent upon the global co-ordination of operational capabilities, which we have separated for discussion purposes into three core processes:

1. *Supply Chain/Network and Logistical Processes:* These include manufacturing, purchasing, transportation, and warehousing processes involved in acquiring, producing, and moving goods and services to wherever in the world the customer wants them. Coordinated global integration of the supply chain requires cooperation between members at a strategic as well as operational level.

2. *The Interaction Process:* One element of the interaction process is to establish and coordinate the activity of cross-functional and geographically dispersed account management teams. One of the most important competencies required at a global level, therefore, is the ability to manage information and communications flows that support this effort.

3. *Collaborative Design Process:* Global markets provide opportunities for product and service extension and adaptation. It is increasingly important that suppliers are able to collaborate with their customers to facilitate not only the development of new global products and services, but also the adaptation of existing offerings to conform to global/local requirements.

Developing GAM processes involves adaptations of a strategic, operational, and relational nature. GAM processes require global marketing channel management, involving organizational adaptations that lead to suppliers becoming more global account focused. The influence of sales and marketing, operational staff, and senior management during the initiation of the GAM process is critical.

An Established and Effective NAM Program
In the Global Account Management Study conducted in 1999, we found that those companies that had successful NAM programs were more likely to implement a global account management program successfully. Some of the reasons for this finding are that NAM programs require significant executive support, focus on value selling and not price, have had a cultural shift from territory (local) selling,

and resource reallocations have been made to meet the needs of critical customers.

Senior Executive Sponsorship

Senior management support for and involvement in the GAM process is an essential, though not sufficient, requirement for the effective implementation of GAM programs. Support for the program must be engendered, not only from the top of the organization but also from all levels of management, from all functional specialties within the firm, and from remote locations as well as headquarters.

> The real name of the game in GAM is executive selling at the most senior level. Account executives sell at operational levels, account managers attempt to sell to middle managers, but the only way this really works and bring us profit is through coordinated efforts where we make the plays at the executive level.
>
> Tom McCarty, Motorola

Developing GAM processes involves major adaptations to the strategies, structures, and systems within organizations. Inherent in these changes are threats to the established order, to areas of control, factional interests, and established cultural perspectives. Senior managers must not merely signal their support for the new program, but must become *entangled* in its implementation if these changes are to be embraced. By this we mean that they must demonstrate that this ties their own future within the organization to the fortune of the program, and their support must be demonstrated and tangible.

Figure 3.1

Initiating GAM Programs

Section 2: GAM Initiation

Once the pre-GAM factors are in place, it is time to focus on the three factors important to ensuring that the GAM program becomes a reality. These three factors are selling the GAM program internally, selecting the global account managers, and defining and selecting the accounts that will become the company's first global accounts.

Internal Selling of the New GAM Program

While senior management support is essential, it is not a sufficient condition of successful GAM implementation. Where GAM is perceived as being the exclusive preserve of senior managers, programs were found to be far less successful. GAM strategies merely driven from the top down lack the *embedded* nature of the operational and inter-organizational elements that characterize successful GAM programs. The aim of senior management should be to secure involvement and commitment to organizational and operational integration at all levels of the organization.

There is a need for wide support within the company from those executives who have the power to sabotage the initiative and from those who are charged with the implementation of the global strategy at local level. In order to achieve this, the program must acknowledge and take account of the various factional interests within the organization.

We have observed a number of initiatives on the part of global account management teams directed towards achieving and sustaining internal support. These initiatives have one thing in common: their emphasis upon the importance of internal communications.

At one company we observed that the global program was given its own logo within the organization. An internal corporate identity was created that was communicated through developing its own Web page and a magazine that was sent to all internal personnel. Both carried success stories that built a corporate-wide perception of the GAM program as being both important within the company and a good initiative to be associated with.

At another company the internal selling process was taken just as seriously as the development of customer relationships strategies within their global *Alliance Account Program*. In the first year of the program's development, hundreds of presentations were made to both customers and internal stakeholders, but for every presentation made to a client organization, five were made internally. In addition, each member of the account team around the world was charged with targeting a number of internal people whose support was thought to be critical to the success of the program. The SVP leading the Alliance Program was charged with developing and sustaining support at Board level. Global account managers at the VP level sought support from their peers in other functional areas of the firm, and managers / franchise owners of individual properties (hotels and conference centers) were targeted for support by members of the global team.

Internal selling of the program must go beyond stressing the corporate benefits of adopting GAM processes and address the specific interests and concerns of these internal players. Country and local SBU managers must be convinced that the proposed changes will help them achieve their own personal and business goals. Internal promotion must also recognize cultural differences between different parts of the organization and address the problem of developing methods of reward and recognition that reflect both national conditions and the contributions made by individuals to the success of the program.

Although the term *global account management* would suggest that the process is essentially concerned with managing external relationships, our research findings suggest that a major component of all successful GAM programs is concerned with managing internal support for the global customer management strategy. Internal support, from both the senior management team and from middle managers, from global headquarters and local field operations, is a fundamental requirement in the early stages of GAM implementation. The management of both the internal and external processes is both iterative and interrelated, but we suggest that in the early stages of development, the major focus of activity should be upon ensuring internal support and the necessary internal systems and processes to support the GAM program.

The Global Account Manager

The global account manager plays a major part in successfully implementing GAM programs. The results of the global account management study found that most current global account managers come from national account manager positions, and although the skills needed for global account management are similar to those of a national account manager, there are some significant differences.

> *I would argue that if you listed all of the skills of a good salesperson and prioritized them and listed all of the skills of a global account manager and prioritized them, what you would end up with is the same list but prioritized differently.*
>
> Hewlett Packard

The role of the global account manager will be discussed in greater depth in later chapters. For the moment, it is interesting to note that while most are drawn from a sales background, selling skills were not rated as the most important attribute they should possess. Selling skills are perceived as a given, while the skills of communication, leadership and team management, and business acumen were considered much more important.

The Top 10 Global Account Manager Competencies:

1. Communication skills
2. Global team leadership and team management skills
3. Business and financial acumen
4. Relationship management skills
5. Strategic vision and planning capabilities
6. Problem solving skills
7. Cultural empathy
8. Selling skills (internal and external)
9. Industry and market knowledge (self and customer)
10. Product/service knowledge

That most global account managers are drawn from within their own organizations, rather than being recruited from outside, reflects the need for them to have a deep understanding of the workings of their own company.

Based upon the GAM Survey results and the evidence drawn from a series of in-depth interviews, we identified three main categories of global account manager competencies. These relate to analytical skills; international awareness and experience; and broader business and commercial skills that may be classed as entrepreneurial and political in nature. These allow them to operate at a much higher strategic level within and between organizations than is usual with national account managers.

When you become a global account manager two things happen. One, the geography gets a lot bigger, and two, the time zones are more intense. So you are not only working around the world but you are also working around the clock.

Elaine Thillen, Xerox

The Definition and Selection of Global Accounts

Many respondents during our research emphasized the importance of developing a clear process for defining and selecting global accounts. Some of the reasons for this have already been discussed when we noted in Chapter Two that striving to provide a global value proposition to a non-global customer was wasteful of resources and likely would fail to deliver real value. There are, however, a number of additional reasons why definition and selection are important.

Customers that are perceived as being of major strategic importance to the company as a whole may not be perceived as important at a regional or country level. Local managers will fight to protect the interests of *their* strategic accounts if they are not convinced of the value of the global account relationship, not only to the company as a whole, but to their own part of the company. One way of minimizing the resistance to the designation of global account status is to remove the selection process from the political arena within the organization.

Selection should be based upon clearly defined criteria that, in simple terms, define the long-term potential of the global relationship and the company's ability to serve the needs of that account. The specific criteria by which global accounts are chosen should be established before individual choices are made. These criteria should be agreed within the company so that when specific accounts are selected the choice is perceived as rational and fair.

Our observations suggest that there will be more companies that could be treated as global accounts than there are resources to serve them. Making the correct choice therefore involves deciding which of the available accounts offer the best return on the resources they will absorb. GAM programs are expensive in terms of the demands they make upon time, money, and personnel, and if returns on this investment are reduced because of poor account selection, it will be difficult to retain support for the overall program. Thus, it is critical to establish a robust selection process.

> It is really important to select your global customers wisely, because those are the ones that should recognize the value given and therefore be willing to pay you back for it.
>
> Gary Silk, Hoffman

Results from the Global Account Management Research Project offer some insights into developing criteria for selecting the global accounts. Two sets of factors need to be considered when selecting global accounts from the portfolio of potential customers. The first is *Operational Factors*, which are generally quantitative, and the second is *Relational Factors*, which tend to be qualitative in nature.

Operational Factors in Selecting Global Accounts:

1. One of company's largest accounts
2. Future sales potential
3. High current sales potential
4. Viewed as technology leaders
5. Perceived as largest company in sector
6. Increasing their expenditures
7. Highest growth in their sector
8. Most profitable customer (for supplier)
9. Offer technology synergy

Criteria relating to the level of present and potential revenue represented by the customer, share of spend, and relative profitability are obviously important. Most companies use these measures together with an assessment of their customers' geographical spread to select their global accounts. A further consideration by some suppliers is the access that the customer provides to new technology or markets.

Few companies, in our experience, have the necessary information to judge account attractiveness based on profitability, but we also believe that this will become an increasingly important criterion as the ability to attribute costs to specific relationships is enhanced by information technology. At present, only suppliers involved in projects-based businesses tend to have the necessary information to make this possible. Most manufacturers measure the profitability of their product portfolio, but few recognize the importance of measuring the profitability of their customer portfolio and have not developed the systems to capture the necessary information.

Even though many of the criteria used to identify and select global customers are understandably quantitative, our research found that the relational aspects of global customer selection are critical for realizing the profit potential of the account. While all companies in our research used quantitative measures in their selection process, the more experienced tended to attach greater weight to qualitative factors. Quantitative measures were viewed as *qualifiers* while the relational factors were perceived as having a far greater impact upon strategy realization. They recognize that successful GAM is dependent upon successful partnering and cultural alignment between client and supplier.

Relational Factors in Selecting Global Accounts:

1. Close current or potential buyer / suppler relationship
2. Collaborators
3. Current or potential strategic alignment
4. Current good relationships already exist

Many decisions to designate a particular account as global are made under the stimulus of competitive pressure. *"If we don't do it, our competitors will!"* While this is a good reason for starting a GAM program, it is not a reliable basis

Table 3.1

Revenue Potential
"Global customers represent significant revenue potential"
Global Account Management programs are primarily aimed at increasing the supplier's share of customer spend and therefore the potentials for increasing business volume and profitability are important in account selection.

Centralized/Co-coordinated Purchasing System
"Our global customers must be moving towards centralized/coordinated decision making processes and be involved in outsourcing and vendor reduction programs"
This was seen as necessary in order to ensure that a common global agreement between the two organizations could be implemented. Without a centralized/coordinated purchasing process the potential for conflicting local arrangements severely prejudices the global agreement. Customers must be able to interact with a similar level of strategic, operational and technical capability across their global operations. Otherwise the value of the global offering will be diluted or lost.

Possesses a Global Mindset
"Global customers demand global agreements and purchasing/supply co-ordination."
If the customer is unable to take strategic and operational decisions globally, they are unlikely to benefit from the global offering of their supplier. Equally it is unlikely that the supplier will find this type of customer profitable.

A Degree of Strategic and Cultural Fit
"Global customers must have the potential to significantly impact on our global objectives and strategies."
Strategic alignment and cultural empathy between global account and supplier is considered to be extremely valuable in facilitating the ongoing development of a global relationship.

Potential for Relational Closeness
"Global customers are actively seeking global supplier alliances."
Softer, less tangible factors play a major part in the development and execution of the global account management process. The ability and willingness to *partner* is seen as a major factor in global account management attractiveness.

Present an Opportunity for Value Creation
"We are looking at accounts that have a migration path that is parallel to the one we have strategically selected for ourselves. We want customers who, down the line, want us to do more than just provide basic products."
The primary objective of many GAM programmes is not to increase revenue through a greater volume of product sales, but to enhance account profitability by offering higher value to the customer through a broader, more comprehensive offering, focused upon the individual global account.

upon which to choose specific global accounts. Global account selection needs to be based upon criteria that support the strategic objectives of the supplier and effect a match between realizable potential and available resources. Some customers are best left to the competition! Most companies in our survey used a variety of criteria that reflected their particular circumstances and the specific relationship under consideration. These criteria are summarized in *Table 3.1*.

The primary objective of the really effective GAM program that we observed is not merely to increase revenue through greater volume of product sales, but to enhance the profitability of the *relationship* through a broader, more comprehensive offering focused upon the needs and potentials of the individual account. As we will discuss later, this is not achieved ultimately through product sales but through the identification of synergistic potential for exploiting the core competencies of both organizations in joint value creation. In order to define and select global accounts, we recommend that the following steps be followed:

1. Establish the criteria by which *your* global, regional, other international account customers may be defined that reflect the overarching strategic objectives that you have established for your global operation.

2. Establish in broad terms the value proposition that each category of customer may require and is capable of receiving and the resources required to meet these needs. This, together with the identification criteria, provides a template against which you can compare individual accounts under consideration for global treatment.

3. Gain organizational buy-in to those criteria *before* you try to identify individual accounts for global treatment.

4. Use the criteria to measure the suitability of individual accounts for global, regional, or international offerings. Each account will need to be judged against the criteria that have been established, which will include their potential for profitable relational growth, your ability to serve them, and the proportion of available resources the relationship will absorb.

5. Create a portfolio matrix that positions global accounts hierarchically in terms of their attractiveness and your ability to serve their needs profitably.

6. Designate those that offer the greatest potential as your global accounts.

Among your portfolio may be companies operating internationally or at a regional level that are not truly global. If they have the potential to significantly influence your long-term strategic direction, they should still be singled out for special treatment within the GAM program. The value proposition they are offered should reflect their ability to receive it and may include help in becoming global operators. By carrying out a thorough analysis of international accounts, you are able to identify those accounts with present and future potential and determine the level of resources that should be allocated to developing relationships with them.

Section 3: Facilitating Factors

Even when a company has the pre-GAM criteria in place from Section One and has accomplished all of the initiatives in Section Two, the likelihood of a successful launch of a GAM program is still in doubt unless three additional factors are implemented. The three factors are concerned with having an effective communication system (both internal and external), a specifically designed reward and compensation system that that engages and supports the global strategy, and the ability to do real-time account planning and reporting.

1. Effective Systems for Communicating Internally / Externally

Communication is a major component of the GAM process. The global account manager is working across many time zones and over great distances, and it is important for them to be able to communicate effectively internally as well as with customers in a timely and responsive fashion. The use of email, voice mail, mobile phones, and other electronic measures allows a global account manager to reach out to customers as well as have customers reach out to them. Since one of the benefits of being a global customer is to have a single point of contact to resolve problems, it is imperative that the global account manager be able to be in contact with customers almost instantly (in some cases), or at least accessible 24 hours a day.

The communication infrastructure is important in order for a global account manager to contact others within their own organization if problems are to be resolved quickly and efficiently. These two communication systems (internal and external) need to be compatible so that a global account manager does not need to waste time retyping or otherwise reproducing information to be communicated to internal personnel or conversely communicating information from internal team members to customers.

> *Information Technology is going to be more and more important.*
>
> *Paul Crunkleton, Eastman Chemical*

The other major infrastructure needed is that of information technology. One of the advantages of being a global customer is being able to share information with suppliers in order to increase efficiency and stimulate creative solutions to current and future problems. Some of the information content required may be specialized reports from the supplier that help the customer reduce costs or increase customer satisfaction, either of which aid in the development of mutual benefits. If the customer and supplier information systems are compatible, the captured information can be used to create value for the customer by giving the knowledge away as part of the supplier's total global offering.

With today's wide variety of technologies and information systems, it is easy to see how there could be incompatibilities between the buyer and seller. If such incompatibilities exist, the potential for mutual benefit is limited. The ability to share information seamlessly is a feature that a supplier and buyer must have if they are to build the relationship on more than simply driving cost out of the supply system. The real value of the global account management program is being able to create future value through collaboration with the customer. The information infrastructure must be compatible with this goal.

2. Reward and Compensation Packages

Early on in the process, attention must be paid to reward and recognition for achievement of objectives within the GAM program. Companies that develop a fair and equitable compensation system that recognizes the multi-level and multi-cultural nature of global account management will improve the productivity of the GAM program and reduce the incidence of conflict or turf wars.

Many companies take existing compensation plans that were developed for local or national accounts programs and simply attempt to apply them in a global context. This is dangerous because it neither recognizes the impact of culture upon the effectiveness of reward programs, nor does it

> *If you have conflicting measurement standards, then the difficulty of supporting and selling a national or global account is going to vary accordingly. What we are trying to do is change the measurement system from local P&L to measurement of the management team around the world. The measurement is based on service levels, productivity, quality, and not just sales/profit. We have made it so that 25% of a branch manager's compensation is tied to global account customer satisfaction rating.*
>
> John Fitzgerald, Fritz Companies

make allowances for the differences that may exist between different local levels of compensation.

Three issues need to be addressed: the reward and compensation packages of the global account managers and their teams, the way in which costs and revenues are allocated between local and corporate operations, and the impact of culture upon the effectiveness of reward systems to motivate.

The impact of salary and bonus levels upon individual performance must be considered. Salary and bonus should reflect both the contributions being made to the global initiative and the prevailing local conditions. High differentials between the remuneration paid to the core global team and the local people charged with delivering the global promise may act as a disincentive.

At an organizational level, country and regional managers are unlikely to support the global initiative unless there is some benefit to them. Where the implementation of the global strategy depends upon the good will of local managers, this must be reflected in the way in which their performance is judged. The attribution of costs and revenue can have a major impact upon how easily GAM is implemented, and some companies take an extremely pragmatic approach through the judicious use of "double counting."

A further consideration is the impact of culture. What may seem an extremely fair compensation package from a North American perspective may be totally unacceptable to people in other parts of the world. Care must be taken to balance the reward given to the team or to the individual, for example, because the effectiveness of either approach will vary between different parts of the world.

> *When we want to get our European sales force to sell more North American products, it is difficult. The General Manager in that country is not graded heavily on selling U.S. products. He is graded on the throughput of his four manufacturing facilities.*
>
> *Ed Bollman, Bussman Corporation*

Treating the cause is the only real way to control the process. Thus, having a comprehensive evaluation / compensation plan developed before embarking on a global account management program is critical. It is only through the use of a new comprehensive plan that problems like double counting/paying, windfall commissions, cannibalization of sales, and loading/delaying sales can be minimized.

3. Account Planning and Reporting Processes
Closely allied to a requirement for effective communication and information technology is the need for an iterative real-time account planning process that links all the members of the account team and allows each of them access to account information and take part in the planning and reporting process.

Far from being an isolated and discrete activity, the planning and implementation of global account strategies is necessarily both a group activity and a continual process, which is heavily dependent upon information.

GAM team members tend to be scattered around the world operating within different parts of the client organization and on different time scales from their colleagues. Information and communications systems support their ability to gather and disseminate client information and to collectively formulate account strategies, implement them in a coordinated fashion, and monitor progress. The rate of change also dictates that strategies are not static but continually subject to revision and update as the situation changes.

The Transition to Global Account Management

The transition from national, international, or even regional to global account management will have a fundamental impact upon the supply organization. Part of the process will be painful as political positions are reconciled or realigned, and as changes are made to existing ways of doing business and their underpinning systems, structures, and processes.

Many of the challenges, however, may be managed through the development of clear strategic objectives and careful planning for their implementation. The initiation of a GAM program will be facilitated by:

- Understanding the pre-GAM conditions
- Generating organizational buy-in to the process

- Recruiting the right global account managers
- Clearly defining and carefully selecting global accounts
- Developing underpinning systems and processes
- Accepting that the process is complex, long term, and demands an ongoing flexibility and acceptance of ambiguity not generally present in national account management

In the following chapters we will consider how companies develop their competencies in global account management in order to create and sustain value propositions for and with their global customers.

CHAPTER IV

Global Supply
Chain Management

Chapter IV: Global Supply Chain Management

Definitions: A Supply Chain is the economic system through which goods and services are developed, produced, and delivered. Supply chains cross-organizational boundaries and embrace products and services from their conception to their final consumption and destruction. Supply Chain Management is the organization of these systems to achieve a competitive return for the business.

Introduction

The operational consequences arising from the development of GAM have a major impact on supply chains. Companies must not only consider their own resources and capabilities when serving their global accounts, they must be able to marshal the resources and competencies of their suppliers, partners, and distributors in ways that support their global account strategies. With products and services being produced and delivered globally, the coordination, control, and development of global performance is a mammoth task, and one that involves extensive third party collaboration and close supplier involvement. For example, the global auto industry depends heavily upon its suppliers for the both the design and the manufacture/assembly of major vehicle assemblies. As a result, vehicle quality is largely dependent on the quality capability of the vehicle's suppliers, while the auto manufacturer's competitive performance is directly affected by any failure by a supplier that is discovered by the consumer. In short, the auto manufacturers carry the risks arising from suppliers' performance, an interdependence that underlines the strategic importance of effective supplier-customer collaboration.

The interdependence between customers and suppliers sets GAM within a *dyadic* or two-party context that is part of the broader network or chain of activities and relationships. Further, with competition often taking place between supply chains, not just individual corporations, GAM can be seen as an important dimension of a total supply chain strategy. In this chapter we explore the nature of supply chain management with a particular emphasis on the operational effectiveness required for the successful delivery of GAM strategies.

Why Is Supply Chain Management Important?

The majority of the resources and assets employed by an organization are vested in their supply chains. For example, the supply chain costs for leading S&P Industrials such as Dell, Wal-Mart, Boeing, and Motorola average eight percent of their total operating costs, with purchase costs accounting for an additional sixty percent of operating costs. Consequently, the leverage impact on profit from improving supply chain cost efficiency is an almost one-for-one relationship, with improvements in areas such as inventory turn, lead-time reduction and unit transport costs making a direct contribution to bottom-line profit. Further, increased efforts to reduce purchase prices have a similar one-for-one impact on profits, leading many purchasers to seek annual price reductions from their suppliers. Increasingly, the pressure to achieve cost reductions has led companies to collaborate in order to achieve economies in transaction costs and interlocking processes. One of the major operational drivers of the GAM process is the desire of suppliers and customers alike to achieve global economies through inter-organizational integration/coordination of process and logistics systems.

In mature markets, new product introduction and improved market share are key requirements for sustaining competitive success. Faced with shortening life cycles for products and services in many sectors such as consumer electrical and electronic goods, pharmaceuticals and healthcare, light engineering, office services, and facilities management, increased attention is paid to product and service innovation, market penetration, and sales growth. In emergent "new economy" industries such as e-commerce, ASP (application service provision), and collaborative management, the emphasis is similarly on innovation and rapid market growth. So, in both "old" and "new" industries, the dominant drivers for supply chain strategy have been found to be rapid product and service innovation and enhanced supply chain coordination through the use of e-business systems.

Coupled with the opportunities afforded by e-business, continuing price pressures imposed by major global accounts on corporations like Procter & Gamble have led many organizations to undertake a major review of their supply chain strategies.

★ **Procter and Gamble**

Facing the need for more frequent low volume deliveries into store, the adoption of everyday low pricing (EDLP), the requirement for suppliers to take a proactive role in managing categories of products, including those supplied by competitors, and the opportunities provided by e-business, P&G has joined forces with its competitors to form *Transora*, a major FMCG Web portal designed to facilitate more collaborative use of logistics resources and improve the retail industry's supply chain efficiency.

Access to global customers demands a global presence, whether through branch offices, agents, distributors, or other third party ventures. Very much the front line of the GAM process, customer-facing operations are responsible for delivering goods and services to the global account, as well as interpreting customer requirements, managing customer service, and contributing to the development of the customer relationship. As the use of Customer Relationship Management (CRM) systems increases as a means of collecting and developing intelligence relating to global account planning, so too will the need to ensure that all front line providers are in tune with the corporate GAM message. As we have already seen in this book, one of the key activities of the GAM is to promote the GAM process within the supply chain. The ability to make an active contribution to GAM and CRM processes is a vital requirement for the distribution side of the supply chain.

Increasing trends in outsourcing as indicated by recent research by PriceWaterhouseCoopers show that for non-direct business processes such as human resource management, information technology/systems, and facilities management, corporations are increasingly outsourcing to a third party. The trend to outsource non-core processes continues. Indeed, this is one of the catalysts for GAM, which will further increase the dependence of organizations on suppliers and subcontractors.

The increased reliance of one organization upon the performance of another has helped to raise the importance of effective management of suppliers, distributors, and partners under the broad heading of supply chain management.

What Is Global Supply Chain Management?

Global supply chain management is primarily concerned with the management of the resources, processes, and capabilities required to deliver specific products and services between organizations, wherever they may interact around the world. Most organizations participate in a number of supply chains by virtue of their portfolio of goods and services. For example, take the case of fashion manufacturer Jaeger, a division of the global thread and garment corporation Coats Viyella. Their range of men's and women's clothing will utilize some common supply chains, notably for thread and accessories such as zippers and buttons. However, the fabric supply chain for men's suits is in most cases different from that of the women's. One important factor in separating the fabric supply chain is related to the behavior of different fabrics under alternative designs. A single-breasted blazer will place very different demands in terms of the dimensional strength of the fabric compared to that of a double-breasted blazer, and consequently, the structure and constitution of the two fabrics will be different, necessitating alternative suppliers. The complexity of dealing with multiple supply chain networks is necessarily increased where the product development, manufacturing, and marketing processes are spread around the world. Global supply chain initiatives strive to manage such complexity by identifying suppliers who can coordinate their own logistical processes across national and regional boundaries in such a way that they complement the customers' own process capability.

Across the supply chain there are exchanges of four different forms of resource: physical resources, information, financial resources, and relationships. We class "relationships" as a resource because relationships between individuals, groups, and organizations have a distinctive form, and because we have found that they play an important role in the development of supply chains.

Figure 4.1 below gives an overview of the types and direction of exchanges that may occur across the supply chain. Typical roles associated with supply chain management are buying, selling, shipping, and marketing, all of which are associated with the resource flows between one organization and another. Buyers deal with suppliers to procure goods and services at competitive prices, and sales people negotiate with customers to secure orders. Such roles are typical boundary-spanning activities. However, global supply chain management is concerned with much more than these boundary-spanning roles, being very much involved with the integration of different organizations' activities through the coordination of people, assets, processes, and resources deployed across national borders throughout the supply chain. It is with supply chain integration that modern organizations are concerned.

Figure 4.1

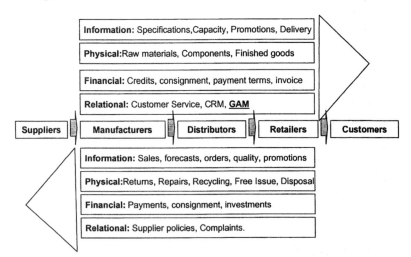

It is fair to say that international supply chain management has been practiced since the dawn of economic activity.

The East-West trading routes for silk, spices, and cotton are all examples of early systems that operated using the type of integrated methods we would recognize today as supply chain management, in which close collaboration and mutual cooperation typify the way in which disparate groups work together. By modern standards, however, these early networks were relatively simple. Today, the increasing globalisation of markets, technology, communications, increasingly demanding customers, and shrinking product life cycles contrive to add levels of complexity that demand continual improvement in the integration of logistical, supply chain, and processing capability.

The operation of supply chains is influenced by three key design decisions areas, which are termed synthesis, synergy, and synchronization.

- *Synthesis* refers to the design of the structure of the supply chain, in terms of the scale, location, technology, and ownership of processes and resources within the supply chain. The alignment of the operations processes across the supply chain has a major part to play in the competitive success of the chain in terms of supporting cost and flexibility requirements.

★ **Dell Computers**

A classic illustration of the impact of supply chain synthesis is that of Dell Computers, which decided to deal with customers directly rather than through retailers or other intermediaries and, as a consequence, gained valuable intelligence about market needs and trends. In addition, they have outsourced much of their product manufacturing to suppliers, thereby minimizing inventory costs and improving their flexibility of response to changes in demand and technical specification.

- *Synergy* refers to the complementary nature of relationships between the parties to the supply chain. Close relationships are seen as often viewed as synergistic, benefiting both parties. We also see that the greater the synergy between parties to the supply chain, the greater the degree of responsibility given to one's partner, supplier, or distributor. Synergy between parties is important for innovation, when new products and services are being developed through collaboration (often called "design chain").

★ Jaguar X-Type and Boeing 777 Design Chains

The successful launch of the Jaguar X-type in February 2001 relied upon the extensive use of suppliers' design resources during its development. Suppliers undertook approximately 40 percent of the design activity, and the X-Type development process depended upon the alignment of suppliers' design strategies with those of Jaguar. Boeing's development of the 777 reflects the full use of the design chain, in which they involved eight of the world's major airlines in setting the functional specifications and enlisted the involvement of subcontractors and system designers in using state-of-the-art CAD. From the project green light in October 1990, it took Boeing's design chain just four years to launch the first flight, and by May 1995 they delivered the first 777 to United.

- *Synchronization* refers to the alignment of supply to demand across supply chain, for example by matching output to demand. Improved synchronization can greatly improve customer satisfaction at the same time as reducing costs; however, attempts to achieve synchronized supply are exacerbated by poor coordination and the existence of a phenomenon called the Bullwhip Effect.

★ **The Bullwhip Effect**

Achieving synchronized product and workflow across a supply chain is hindered by the existence of the Bullwhip or Forrester Effect. In simple terms, this describes the impact of minor fluctuations in activity at one end of the supply chain (such as a few percentage point changes in consumer demand), which results in major amplitude of variation several stages farther down the supply chain. Typically, the prime causes of the supply chain volatility are time lags between demand and supply at each stage in the chain and the intervention of localized planning and scheduling rules. Efforts to remove the Bullwhip Effect include the adoption of category management of supply by retailers and the increased deployment of Collaborative Planning, Forecasting, and Replenishment (CPFR) amongst logistics providers. While these initiatives have had considerable success in the U.S. and Europe, there may be considerable obstacles to overcome when introducing CPFR in cultures that exhibit quite different attitudes towards time and bureaucratic procedures.

Strategic Supply Chain Management

Effective management of the supply chain represents a major area of strategic importance for any organization, not least because the main strategic opportunities lie at the boundaries of the organization. Leveraging value in the market place and employing the distinctive capabilities of suppliers and partners are key factors in the strategic success of the corporations we have studied. Strategic supply chain management is concerned with the identification and exploitation of these opportunities.

In this book we are interested in how companies respond to their important customers. What we have seen is that in order to transform major customers into global accounts, it is necessary to build closer relationships based on developing and then satisfying customer needs. It is clear from our research that the translation of customer needs into operational performance requires a degree of reconciliation between the capabilities of the supply chain and the centralized and dispersed requirements of the global account.

To understand the nature of this strategic reconciliation, we distinguish between *operational* reconciliation and *relational* reconciliation.

Operational Reconciliation relates to the clear determination of the performance required from production and delivery processes across the supply chain in order to support the organization's competitiveness. Supply chain operations contribute to competitive performance through their ability to meet the specific objectives of the business in terms of the five basic performance objectives of cost, quality, speed, dependability, and flexibility. Thu, for the GAM it is not only critical that are the operational objectives for the global account are clearly determined, but also that these objectives both are communicated throughout the supply chain and are feasible given the nature and constraints of supply chain processes.

Relational Reconciliation is determined by the power balance, the degree of trust, and closeness of relationships between the partners to the supply chain. These facets of the customer-supplier relationship have a significant role to play in the development of competitive supply chain performance. In broad terms, the nature of relationships has a direct bearing on the extent to which an organization will outsource increased responsibility to its suppliers. The closer the relationship—and, by implication, the greater the equity of power and degree of trust—the greater the extent of growth of value by the provision of outsourced activities by the supplier. It is this link between the closeness of relationships and the success of the GAM program that we have been examining in this book so far.

> Wherever our customers may be, they want us to do exactly the same thing in China as we do in Massachusetts.... When we set up a new facility near a customer, they know that we already have satisfied their needs somewhere in the world with virtually identical facilities to those that we are bringing to a new location.
>
> James Buonomo, President of Nypro, Asia Pacific

The Impact of Global Supply Chain Management on GAM

Our research, and that of others, has shown how supply chains are physically lengthening in industries as diverse as foodstuffs, pharmaceuticals, electronic components, financial services, facilities management, and manufacturing. The use of foreign sources of supply, the increased reach to global customers, the adoption of integrated management systems, and continued industry consolidation are key drivers for the globalization of supply chains. As a result, an integral part of the GAM process is the marshaling of supply chain resources across international boundaries. This involves not only physical resources such as manufacturing or processing technologies, but also effective use of the relationships that exist between members of the supply chain.

Our study of global account management showed that effective GAM programs require alignment between the account strategy and the capabilities of the global supply chain. In particular, organizations such as H-P, IBM, Nypro, Moore Corporation, Procter & Gamble, Philips, Hitachi, and SC Johnson, we found that a very strong relationship between effective GAM and clear supply chain developments highlighted the dependence of their GAM program success on their development of an integrated global supply chain.

The success and effectiveness of GAM performance is strongly correlated with both a global logistics operation and global manufacturing strategies. Delivering a consistent quality service to the global account depends upon the integration of these functions within the GAM program.

> In Marriott's Global Alliance program, it is critical for us to ensure that sales, logistics, operations, service, and support are all aligned with the global account strategy.
>
> Steve Richard, Marriott

CHAPTER V

Organizational Structure

CHAPTER V: ORGANIZATION STRUCTURE

Introduction

GAM strategies are essentially concerned with creating value for and with global clients through the coordination of sales, services, operations, logistics, information systems, and ultimately, strategic integration worldwide. It therefore follows that the organizational structure that underpins GAM should facilitate, rather than impede, that process.

The key task is to ensure that the global promise is delivered at a local level, that the customer receives the same level of value at their outlying facilities as they do at headquarters. GAM programs demand organizational change. They require the establishment of global teams and the reconfiguration of existing structures to facilitate local delivery anywhere in the world of the global offering. Where

Global suggests some degree of coordination, integration, and cooperation. Take the example of two one-year-old babies. If you place them on a mat together, they don't play with each other, they parallel play. They co-exist, but the interaction between them is fairly passive. That reflects a company that is multi-national. Then take the example of eleven men on a football field, and you expect much higher levels of coordination and cooperation. Global implies a lot more cooperative teaming.

Mike Cohn, Hewlett Packard

the global vision has not been effectively communicated throughout the organization, organization structures are unlikely to recognize or allow the effective management of the organizational complexity and cultural diversity implicit in a global operation.

Concepts of Best Practice

Elements of what represents current best practice in GAM are well understood by some practitioners. Fred Schindler of IBM, speaking at the 1999 SAMA Conference, suggested some of the elements of a successful GAM organization.

First, he stressed the importance of the program being developed at corporate level and with the support of a senior executive as champion. Second, the global account manager role should be exclusively global in order to avoid them becoming embroiled in local politics, with local national account managers assigned to local customer facilities. Third, the global account manager should have authority over the global team and be positioned in the corporate hierarchy such that this authority is reinforced.

Drawing upon these observations and others from our research, the ideal structure for a GAM program is one that includes the overall responsibility for the GAM program being in the hands of a senior executive who reports directly to the CEO.

Senior management support for the GAM program was the single most mentioned requirement for success. Positioning the senior manager of the GAM program at corporate level sends out a message to the rest of the organization that the board is taking this seriously. Important as senior management support is, however, it is not sufficient. In addition, there needs to be buy-in from all levels of the organizational hierarchy, particularly at country or regional manager level.

Many companies find it difficult to move from concept to implementation of GAM programs because of the difficulty in realigning, and even more so in replacing, existing organizational structures.

Barriers to Organizational Change

The difficulties are easy to understand. Historically, major multinational companies have been successful precisely because they organized themselves around product groups rather than customers and focused profit responsibility within geographical regions. They have emerged as highly decentralized international organizations, characterized by powerful silos of influence dominated by country or regional managers. Despite a growing recognition by many thought leaders that companies operating in this manner must change radically in order to meet the demands of their global customers, the reality is that there are often massive cultural, organizational, and political barriers to the implementation of those changes. Attempts to implement new organizational structures to facilitate integration and coordination on a global scale pose a threat to the power and the pockets of the very people who can make or break the global initiative.

The Questions Remain:

- How should the GAM process be organized?
- Should the GAM program be managed at corporate level or be delegated to individual countries or regions (Europe, North America, etc.)?
- Should global account managers be located at the customer HQ or at corporate HQ?

- Should the GAM program be established as a separate business unit or should it be overlaid upon existing organizational structures?

The answer is that it depends. It depends upon the specific situation faced by individual companies, the demands and capabilities of their customers, and their own degree of global sophistication.

Approaches to GAM Organization

We have observed a number of different GAM organizational and reporting structures during our research. The three levels of the GAM process (Getting Started, Developing the Competencies, and Sustaining the Effort) within selling organizations relate to the management of strategic direction, individual account management, and the delivery of the value proposition at a local level. These elements of the process vary in the degree to which they are centralized or decentralized, and in the degree to which they are integrated with, or superimposed upon, existing organizational structures.

At one extreme, GAM programs may be managed exclusively from the supplier corporate HQ employing executives and sales people dedicated solely to global clients and operating quite separately from the company's country or regional operations. In these instances, the GAM program team operates as an intermediary channel to market and may act as a "super customer" in its own right. The primary benefit of this structure is that of coordination. It also has the merit of demonstrating senior management commitment to the importance of the GAM program. Unfortunately, it is an expensive solution that requires the duplication of resources at a local level in order to implement the global strategy. Where existing local resources are commandeered for use by the global team, it will tend to produce conflict with local managers and may result in a concerted effort to sabotage the global initiative because it is perceived to threaten local interests.

The second extreme solution might be for responsibility for global account management to be devolved entirely to the country or regional managers in whose territory the customer HQ is located. The benefit in this instance is that political problems are avoided, but this happens at the expense of global coordination. Nevertheless, we have observed that where the power of country or regional silos is very pronounced, the responsibility for developing global strategies has been devolved to local managers. This is often followed, with varying degrees of success, by attempts to integrate those locally developed strategies worldwide through an appeal by the corporate HQ to the enlightened self-interest of other local (country or regional) managers.

Figure 5.1: Alternative Organizational and Reporting Structures

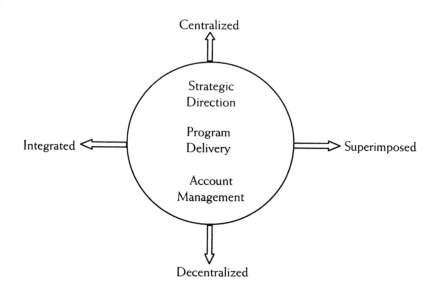

Each company appears to evolve slightly different solutions to these challenges, with some adopting extremely pragmatic approaches that adapt to the needs of the customer and the existing realities of their own organizations. In the cases that are presented below, as with the vast majority of cases we explored during our research, the strategic focus and the driving force of the GAM program is provided by senior members of the firm's management team. These are people who are close to or have positions on the Board, or who report directly to the CEO.

At operational levels, we have observed similar levels of diversity. Some *field* global account managers report directly to a corporate executive who is responsible for the GAM program that is located at HQ. We have observed dual reporting systems to corporate and regional or country managers, and we have seen structures where the global account managers report to their local sales directors or country managers. Different levels of integration with existing structures also exist. In some instances the GAM team is a separate operating unit, while in other cases members of the team have dual responsibility for global and local functions.

We provide the following cases in an attempt to illustrate some of the approaches that we have observed.

Four Examples of GAM Organization

The Case of Dun & Bradstreet[1]
The number of global accounts managed by Dun & Bradstreet grew from 10 to 100 between 1995 and 1999 when

---

[1] This case is based upon material presented at the 35th SAMA Conference "Global Forum Presentation" 1999

50% of these accounts were situated in the U.S., 35% in Europe, and 15% in APCLA (Asia-Pacific, Canada, and Latin America). The corporate structure of the company mirrored these regional markets with each of the regions having its own president and each country a general manager. The structure was hierarchical, with all business functions **reporting upwards.**

Rather than establish the global operation as a separate business unit, the global account management organization was overlaid upon and integrated with the existing local / regional structure. There were two reasons for this. First, a great deal of infra-structural support existed at regional level that could be used to support the new global strategy, and duplication would have been costly. Second, by continuing to book business locally it was hoped that resistance to the program from local people would be avoided.

The only new resources provided were the Global Business Executive Vice President (EVP) based in Portugal, three Regional Global Customer Managers (RGCMs), and, reporting to them, 40 newly appointed Local GCMs. In addition, there were a small number of functional specialists providing marketing, IT, and financial services support.

The location of the EVP Global Business in Portugal was a major statement by D&B in order to emphasize that the global program was not an ethnocentric U.S. initiative. As a member of the senior management team within D&B, the global EVP also reported directly to the CEO, again underpinning the importance of the initiative.

The RGCMs were promoted from senior sales manager roles within each region and chosen for their enthusiasm and commitment to the global concept. Local GCMs were generally made responsible for servicing a number of global accounts. They might have responsibility for only global issues, only local issues, or both issues relating to that customer. They might be located at the Regional HQ or in the field, and they may report to the D&B Global Division alone or have dual reporting responsibility. A critical factor is perceived to be the senior management support provided to GCMs and their empowerment to act on behalf of the customer.

D&B has recognized the value of using their existing regional/local expertise and existing organizational structures to facilitate the implementation of the global strategy, while also avoiding the potential hazard of alienating existing power bases within the regions.

The Case of Xerox[2]

Xerox is an example of another company that has attempted to build its GAM program into the existing sales force structure. Xerox has a field engagement model, called a Customer Business Unit (CBU). Dave Potter of Xerox explained their operation in the following way:

> There are 37 (CBUs) in the United States. That is the way we go to market with the direct sales people. There are 8 CBUs in Germany, 7 in France, and 6 or 7 in the U.K. So if a customer deals with Xerox, they are dealing with the CBU whether they are in Singapore or Seattle. That base for the customer is quite recognizable and people think, 'You guys are everywhere.' It's like a McDonald's: they are familiar with how we operate and they know how to deal with us. One aspect of this whole thing is standardization; we are duplicating successes on a worldwide basis.

---

[2] This case is based upon conversations with David Potter of Xerox Corporation during research for this book.

At Xerox all Senior Vice Presidents have global account responsibility. At the country level, global account managers are sales managers with additional responsibility for three or four global customers. They are appointed based on their closeness to the customers' global HQ and are expected to travel to visit the customer's remote locations. The global account manager coordinates with the CBUs in order to ensure that global customers receive the attention and service levels they require. Interestingly, the reward system for local sales people does not reflect the success of the global account relationship worldwide, and their involvement seems to be based upon the relationship that the global account manager has developed with the CBUs in their role as sales managers.

Well, I think that after ten years the global programs have gained general management support. We have got a network of people in place to take care of these customers. Many of the global account managers have been with us for twenty years. Probably the average tenure is more than ten. They've built up a network of contacts that lets them get things done. You've got my organization with five or six people who are constantly bombarding people with: "This is what the global customers want; this is what we need to do." I just came back from Singapore and Tokyo where I met with the President of Asia-Pacific and the President of Fuji Xerox, and basically I said to them at the very beginning of the meeting, "I am here on a lobbying mission. I am lobbying on behalf of these global customers and have come to ask you to do things on behalf of these customers." They smiled and said, "We understand." Then I went on to tell them things that I wanted to ask them to do and questioned their input and that sort of thing, and hopefully got their agreement. So that some time in the future, if I have to go back to them because I've got a problem in Taiwan, I can.

The role of the global account manager appears to be one of lobbying within Xerox on behalf of the customer, using the contacts built up over long years with the company to enlist the support of senior executives and local sales people alike.

In the case of both Dun & Bradstreet and Xerox, the GAM structure is integrated into the broader sales force structure. They both represent a degree of compromise and both use global specialists to perform a number of additional tasks. While the global account manager's primary responsibility may be to the global client, they are also expected to provide broader organizational support wherever that may be needed, whether at a global or local level.

The Case of Hoffman-Schroff HS Systems[3]

A more structured approach was adopted by HS Systems when they began their GAM program in 1998. A new global customer management organization was created from within the International Sales Division. This comprised Executive Sponsorship from two senior executives within the company, the Global Customer Projects Team, the Global Customer Steering Committee, Global Account Leaders, and Local Global Account Managers.

Initially five global customers were identified: one in Asia, one in Europe, and three in the United States. Overseen by the Global Projects Team, which set the overall strategy, the role of the Steering Team was to review account strategies, secure worldwide executive management commitment for the program, and remove internal barriers. They were made responsible for defining the GAM strategy and process, developing systems and guidelines, selecting

---

[3] This case was prepared using material presented at the 35th SAMA Conference "The Global Account Management Panel" 1999

target accounts, and selecting account leaders.

Global Customer Leaders were positioned close to the customer parent location. They reported to the Steering Committee and were made responsible for the following:

- Coordinating the account interface
- Identifying sales growth opportunities at the customer parent location
- Developing the account sales plan and strategy
- Facilitating the flow of information about the account
- Updating the Steering Committee on customer activity and account management effectiveness

Global Customer Managers were appointed to cover customer remote locations reporting to the U.S. via their individual Global Customer Leaders. These customer managers were charged with identifying sales opportunities at customer remote locations, developing an understanding of customer needs, and identifying and supporting incremental business and resources at all customer locations.

This whole structure was supported by the development of a Global Customer Database to facilitate the exchange of account information, the development of customer account profiles, and the identification and management of individual client related projects. The Hoffman-Schroff structure is set out in **Figure 5.2**.

The HS Systems approach represents a situation where the GAM structure is both centralized and superimposed. The GAM program here operates independently of the regional sales and marketing programs and focuses upon a very few customers who are given specialized treatment by a specialist GAM team. Its effectiveness relies heavily upon the political skills of the Steering Committee members in gaining regional executive support and overcoming the barriers to its implementation.

At the time of launching the program, although they had a product range that had been designed to meet customer needs in both North America and Europe, there was no truly global offering, and they did not perceive themselves as a global company. The establishment of the Global Customer Program as a separate project may therefore be viewed as an attempt to initiate the process of globalization within their own organization through focusing upon the needs of a very small group of customers with whom global competencies could be developed. The initiative offered further potential for learning to develop total systems solutions for this select group of customers in a relatively protected environment through the development of in-house competencies and through collaborative partnerships with other suppliers.

Figure 5.2: HS Systems Global Customer Management Organization

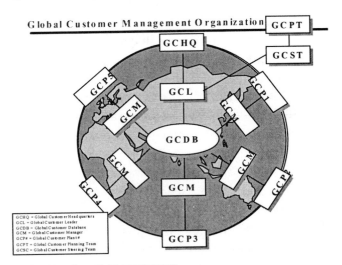

Wilson (1998) "Global Customer Management Panel", Proceedings of the 35th Annual SAMA Conference. Orlando, Florida

The Case of the European Logistics Company

This case traces the changes that have occurred to the global account management program within a major European headquartered logistics company (LC). It shows how organizational structures need to adapt to keep pace with changing market circumstances and customer demand.

The company grew as a highly decentralized document transfer organization with strong regional (Europe, Africa, Asia Pacific, etc.) autonomy, and with a few exceptions, this reflected the case with the majority of their customers. The exceptions were six major banks, customers that were each demanding a global service that would reflect their own degree of global systems integration. These customers were highly centralized with the HQ authority to impose global agreements upon their remote operations.

In response to their customers' demands, LC established a small, dedicated team to exclusively serve this group of customers, led by a senior executive reporting directly to the CEO. Six global account managers were positioned alongside each bank's HQ in order to manage their business separately. All other business with other customers remained with the regional operations of LC.

When LC expanded the range of services they offered to include parcels delivery, they found a growing number of customers demanding global solutions in terms of pricing, value added beyond the core service, and systems harmonization. Twenty-five additional global accounts were identified and an organizational structure was developed that integrated their management into the regional operations.

The nearest regional office to the customer HQ provided the Global Account Manager. The appointee was drawn from the region's group of senior managers and reported directly to the regional sales director. The global account managers were charged with working with global account

97

managers from other regions in order to serve the customer's remote facilities. Global account managers were established in Europe, Africa, Latin America, the United States, and Asia-Pacific, and a virtual global team was evolved to coordinate sales, marketing, support, IT, billing, and customer service. This became known as the Focused Customer Team.

This second iteration was very successful in that it consolidated relationships with a number of customers who wanted inter-regional and, often, global service provisions. As a result of delegating responsibility for these new global accounts to regional level, there was still a tendency for some people to act relatively parochially in the interests of "their" region rather than in the overall interests of the global program. This was also due in part to the way in which business was counted. The region booking the business received the revenue while the region of delivery incurred the cost. This would not have caused a problem were the levels of booking and delivery relatively equal between regions, but LC had a much stronger market position in Europe, Africa, and the Far East than in the U.S. where many of their global customers were exporting to. The United States, doing more deliveries on behalf of other regions while not generating similar levels of revenue because of its relatively poor market position, had real difficulty in resourcing their part of the global focused team program. This and one other factor gave rise to the third iteration of the GAM program at LC.

The other factor was the acknowledgement that by working closely with global accounts from a number of different industries, LC had developed considerable market knowledge and expertise in supply chain and logistics management that was industry specific. This knowledge could be applied to provide value-added offerings to a far broader global client base if it could be managed effectively.

In response to these two factors, a third way was found. The next layer of thirty global accounts was identified, and they were managed through the establishment of a separate organization with full P&L responsibility, an Independent Business Unit (IBU). Under the control of a Global Director, this initiative is headquartered in the United States, because that is where LC wishes to grow the business by focusing upon American-headquartered global clients. The IBU consists of a number of dedicated support teams focusing upon individual global accounts and spread across the regions to service remote customer locations. Each region has a regional IBU Global Director with teams of global account managers segmented by industry and dedicated to individual clients. In addition, Industry Sector Managers, who will coordinate the activities of the global account teams within their industry and facilitate the sharing of knowledge and expertise, will take a lead role. The ultimate aim in adopting this structure is to capture and extend specialized industry-specific expertise and knowledge in order to enhance the ability of LC to act as value adding consultant to their clients in the field of supply chain management and process reengineering. That's an awful long way from delivering packages!

What Can We Learn From These Cases?

These four cases illustrate a number of distinct approaches to the problem of GAM organization that lie between the extremes of centralized or decentralized, integrated or superimposed structures.

In line with the observations of Fred Schindler, in each of the cases the initiative for the GAM program came from the highest levels within the organization. There is an absolute need for the program to be seen as being of paramount strategic importance to the future of the firm. To that extent, all the cases display some degree of centralization. Having said that, a number of alternative approaches to structuring the account management team have been observed.

Early attempts to develop an organizational structure to support GAM initiatives tend to be centralized and superimposed over existing structures. They tend to involve few people and focus upon small numbers of customers. Local delivery of the global offering, where it relies upon the application of local resources, is often dependent upon the political and networking skills of the global account manager in gaining support from local management. In the early stages of the program, this may be seen as a low risk strategy that attempts to use a small, dedicated team to achieve quick wins that provide the stimulus for rolling the program out into the rest of the organization. The fact that the teams are often located at corporate headquarters also adds political clout in those all-important early days.

> In order to get the global message across, both to customers and to your own people, you rely very, very heavily on how your organization is structured. If the GAM program is part of the corporate structure that spans the other entities (functional specialists and remote facilities), then you get very little push back. Where the global account manager is outside the corporate structure, maybe located away from headquarters, then the likelihood is there will be push back. The point is that remote global account managers get embroiled in the politics of the local operations.
>
> Respondent to GAM Survey

An alternative approach adopted where the "silo" effect is very marked is to devolve responsibility for global account management to the country or regional level. This approach was one that was adopted by Motorola in the early days of their GAM program.

★ **Motorola** developed over two decades as a highly decentralized, worldwide, product group structured enterprise. As their customers consolidated and the importance of consistency increased, there was a realization that the company must change. Nevertheless, the realities of the culture that underpinned the existing organization. As early as 1991, the importance of developing global strategic capabilities was recognized, but so was the importance of being able to deliver effectively at a regional level. Attempts to impose a global strategy, or to establish a separate global structure, may have met with resistance from the powerful regional operations. Recognizing the challenge of coordinating the activities of powerful regional operations, each region was encouraged to develop strategies which span the business units and which are developed in conjunction with those businesses.

While both these approaches may be useful in the early days when it is important to test the viability of the program at relatively low cost, the long-term objective must be to achieve integration at two levels. There must be clear commitment to a common global strategy on the part of all those people interacting with the global customer. That implies a degree of strategic coordination, if not centralization. There also must be integration at an operational level that facilitates the seamless delivery of the global offering worldwide. This objective is unlikely to be achieved without the active support of local service providers, whether they report directly to the senior Global Account Manager or have split reporting responsibility.

As programs mature, we observe the development of more complex organizational structures. Some organizations perpetuate the separateness of the GAM organization, placing dedicated sales and support teams around their customer operations that report directly to a corporate level global account manager. Others attempt to integrate the GAM process with the wider sales and service organization at a local level and have dual reporting structures whereby the local account manager may report to both a local manager and to the global account team head.

While the core role of the global account manager is to provide a single point of contact from which the competencies of the global supplier may be leveraged for the benefit of the customer, the major duty is to ensure responsiveness and overcome organizational barriers to the process. What specific organizational structures are adopted depends upon the specific circumstances faced by the individual company.

GAM structures must interact with other functional areas within the firm and reflect the global operations of the customer. Existing organizational structures tend to configure around products, technologies, functional specialism, geographical territory, or some combination via a matrix structure. The key characteristic of global account management structures is that, ideally, they should configure around customers. Two factors constrain the achievement of this ideal. One is the strength of commitment to existing structures within the supplier organization; the other is the number of customers with different and potentially conflicting requirements. Although the idea may be to achieve operational/strategic fit by mirroring the global account's systems and processes, you may have 50-100 accounts which all have their own ideas about how they want their suppliers to interface with them. Some companies have the power to dictate to their suppliers the level of coordination and degree of access, specifying the metrics by which they measure performance worldwide. Others are more flexible and willing to be led by their suppliers. What emerges from these observations is the need to segment global clients and to be proactive in developing generic internal systems and processes to provide a minimum threshold level of access and support, together with custom-made systems and processes and dedicated teams to meet individual account needs.

Where to locate global account management teams is perhaps less problematic, as there is widespread support for locating near the customer with the proviso that senior level global account managers are positioned near the top levels of their own organizational hierarchy. The question of how effectively global account management teams serve global customers is an issue more of management ability, style, and whether there is a culture of cooperation that supersedes parochial political interests. A final word from a respondent from Motorola highlights the two most important elements of an effective GAM team structure: internal coordination and commitment to the process, and flexibility.

With global accounts, if you're not in the total solutions business, you're not going to make money. So you need to involve everyone to deliver service: marketing, systems integration, consulting support, IS, EDI interface, manufacturing.

Where you have a customer with a need in an area where you're not that strong, then you set up a distribution partnership. You make any agreements you need to make with that channel partner to ensure the customer gets the service they need to get. More like a joint venture or an alliance than a dealer agreement. Motorola

CHAPTER VI

Developing GAM Competencies

CHAPTER VI: DEVELOPING GAM COMPETENCIES

In this chapter we examine:

- **The impact of company-wide systems on GAM**
- **The impact of company processes on GAM**
- **The impact of company structure on GAM**

Introduction

We have seen that there is an enormous amount of work and commitment needed just to start a global account management program. This chapter will focus on the issues needed to ensure that the global account program remains viable and functional within the company. Many of the issues have already been introduced and discussed Chapter Three, however, there is considerable more attention needed if the global account program is to be successful in the long run. There are numerous examples of initial success followed by failure due to the lack of improving the initial structures and processes.

In 1999, the CEO of a mid-sized company called the manager of the global account program into his office. The CEO told the global manager that the only reason for the meeting was to immediately dismantle the six-month-old global account program. The global managers were to be immediately assigned to other areas. The CEO said that they had given it a good shot but the results were not justifying the expenses. The global manager reflected back on this experience and identified several areas that might have caused the early withdrawal of support. First, the level of executive support was very thin in that only the CEO was championing the program. Second, the company culture was one of competition between areas within the company. Third was the absence of systems like information, measurement, and global capabilities. Any of these alone would pose a major threat to a global account program's long-term survival.

This example (which we expand upon in the next chapter) illustrates how fragile the existence of a global account program can be even after it is implemented. Care and attention must be taken to ensure that even for successful global account programs to endure they must not presume that what worked initially will necessarily work for long. Thus it is important for global managers and top executives to continue to build and modify company structures, systems, and processes so that they can support the global account program for future success.

Our living in a time of fast-paced change makes it even more important to pay attention to the structures, systems, and processes that can help improve the company's ability to compete in the global marketplace. The order of presentation of the structures, systems, and processes is not designed to imply any relative importance. Instead, the order is relatively unimportant since the issues are not linear but are interrelated.

The topics covered in this chapter are:

- Manufacturing and logistical capabilities
- Account planning processes
- Measurement issues
- Information systems
- Communications

These are followed by a discussion about how reporting systems, reward and recognition systems, and managing perception of the global account management program within the company are improved when the proper systems are in place.

Logistical Capabilities

Just because you have a plant in Saudi Arabia does not mean that the plant can handle the volume being created.
Eric Mason, Werner Ladders

The quotation above illustrates just one of several manufacturing/logistical issues that must be addressed if the global account management program is to be sustained. Senior executives as well as global account managers and their teams need to understand the current and future capabilities of their worldwide operations to deliver product or services to remote or isolated locations. The sheer size of some orders that can be generated with a global customer can place a severe strain on production capabilities of the company. This in turn can have an impact on production costs and the company's relationship with other customers. Just because you have a presence in a country or region does not mean that you can handle large new orders. This is where coordination between the global team and others within the company can prevent embarrassing problems that arise when backorders occur and promises made to other companies are not kept.

Another issue brought out in the research is that companies may not be able to have a specific physical presence (manufacturing, assembly, or distribution) in every location where the customer is located in the world. While there are obvious advantages in terms of speed of response, control, and quality assurance, there are also limitations in terms of finance, personnel, and the level of potential sales that may act to block a company presence in specific locations. That does not mean that your global customers have to look elsewhere to find a supplier. What some companies have done to ensure their customers a reliable supply of products and services is to build alliances with other companies in those specific locations. For example, Fritz Companies did not have a distribution facility in Africa, and one of their global customers had set up a facility there. Instead of heavily investing in a new facility that would only be used for the global customer (an inefficient use of capital), Fritz Companies partnered with a local company to take care of the global customer's needs in that location. Fritz Companies handled the reliability and quality issue by researching the company to find out if they met Fritz's standards and then visiting the location for a final review.

One of the reasons that global account status is so attractive to customers is the fact that they can demand and get consistent quality no matter what the location. It is imperative that companies either develop the capabilities in-house or outsource to obtain the capabilities to meet the needs of global customers. That includes issues like new product development, delivery, warehousing, or other aspects that assist the customer in gaining a competitive advantage in their markets.

Thus, it can be seen that there are multiple issues that must be addressed if the global account management program is to continue in an ever-changing environment.

Information and Communication Systems

Very few firms, including our own, have one common global system.
                    John Fitzgerald, Fritz Companies

Information and communication systems are a company-wide issue but are particularly important to global teams due to time and distance problems. The company infrastructure in terms of both communication and information (data) transfer is critical because it must be sufficient to support multiple platforms that may be used by team members in different parts of the world, while at the same time being cost effective for the company. E-mail is a good example of how technology can hinder rather than help if not properly installed and maintained. This is especially true when e-mail is being used to transfer written material. If all systems are not compatible, it requires the participants at remote locations to either retype or otherwise enter the information into their system before it can be used.

In situations like that, it less likely that information will be useful since people will not want to take the time or put forth the effort to reenter the information or data. It is not expected that a global account manager is to be a technical expert, but it does behoove the global account manager and global team members to have the ability to identify potential disconnects between different information and communications systems. This means that global account managers and team members need a basic understanding of the differences between various technology systems. For example, they may need to understand the difference between TCP and IP, or JPEG and bitmap, if they are to be able to ensure proper communication and transfer of information within their own company and between the customer and their company.

Information systems are also important to a company because of the impact on the reporting systems. For example, it is important to know how much a specific global customer purchases at every location and when those purchases occurred. In the past this has been a problem since some countries were not as sophisticated as the U.S. in capturing sales information. However, with the recent increase in Internet business transactions, the information can be captured and used to provide realistic and meaningful reports no matter where the customer is located. These reports can be used for analysis (account planning) and for evaluation (rewarding).

Account Planning Process

In Chapter Three, the discussion about global accounts was focused on selecting those that offered the most opportunity for success. Our research found that six of the selection criteria were used by almost 25 percent of the sample when companies were identifying potential global accounts. Those areas are, in descending order of importance:

1. High Current Sales Volume
2. Viewed as Technological Leader
3. Largest Customer in Sector
4. Increasing Their Expenditures
5. Highest Growth in Sector
6. Most Profitable Customer

In this section the discussion will focus on two levels of account specifications. First, the macro level revisits the identification and selection process to ensure that the current mix of accounts is still correct. It may be necessary to add new accounts or abandon some of the established accounts so that the overall account mix fits the company strategy and capabilities, while making sure the customers provide for sufficient current and future business.

On this level, it is important for a company to have the correct mix of global accounts in order to maximize profitability. The circumstances that initially placed a company as a global customer may have changed. For example, a company has been designated a global account due to its increasing expenditures in the company's field. However, the global account has retrenched its spending and may no longer be a viable or profitable company to designate as a global customer. The mix of global companies may also depend on the sheer number of companies being served. Companies that have too many or incorrectly selected global accounts run the risk of damaging their image as well as their profitability. Their image can be affected because the prestige associated with being a global account is diminished when so many others have the same status.

Throwing resources (global account management requires larger resources) at too many companies can hurt profitability. Hewlett Packard has learned this lesson. At one point in the 1990s, HP had over 200 accounts classified as global. Upon examination, it was found that many of the companies could be better served without being a global account. HP then went about reclassifying their global accounts and ended up with about 20 truly global accounts. Thus, by matching company resources to customer potential and needs, HP was able to improve profitability and increase customer satisfaction.

A key correlation appears to be between the customer's perception of how well we understand their business and whether or not the relationship is right.

Mike Cohen, Hewlett Packard

The other side of the coin is that companies who have too few or no global accounts face opportunity losses, where other companies can capitalize on their absence. In this type of situation, a company can lose its position as a supplier because a competitor has treated the customer as a global account, which better suits their needs. Global account selection can also be based on a defensive position (to prevent the lose of customers). In either case, the selection of the appropriate number and the appropriate customers to participate in a global account program is key.

On the micro level, the issues are about how to move an established relationship with a current global account further and thereby gain a competitive advantage over competitors. Here the global account management team needs to have a system by which they arrive at specific targets for each global account that reflects customer goals and potential synergies. The account planning system should include communication mechanisms, information capabilities, and regular meetings (via phone, e-mail, videoconferencing, etc.) that can be used to brainstorm, analyze, and strategize to complete the planning process.

All team members need information so that every aspect of the global account can be considered in developing objectives and plans to move the account forward. For example, if a global account manager unilaterally determined the objectives for a global account without having access to information about a local strike in a particular country, the sales projections obtained from achieving the objectives may be incorrect. Or, if there were information on a new competitor that was making inroads in an account but was not know to the global team, the impact could have a drastic impact on future endeavors with that company. It is difficult for the global account manager and top management to accurately plan the future with a global customer if information is lacking or late in arriving.

Just having information is not enough. It is necessary for the global team to meet to facilitate all members being involved in the planning and analysis sessions. By having all or most members of the global team in a real-time meeting, it is possible to make geometric gains because team members can build on each other's comments and issues. Again, the use of technology has reduced the need to physically be together. Instead, other real-time systems (e.g., instant messaging using computers, video conferencing, telephone conference calls) are used to eliminate the time-delayed nature and expense of people who live and work in different parts of the world meeting physically. Thus, scheduling meeting times for the team is critical in that some of the members will always be asked to participate at an inconvenient time. The best solution is to schedule meetings that rotate the people who have to get up at 3 AM to participate. However, just scheduling the meeting times is not sufficient. The team members have to see a value in their being a part of the team. They need to know that their ideas and insights will be taken seriously and not just acknowledged then ignored. Participation in a real-time virtual meeting provides teams the opportunity to provide input and get immediate feedback as to its usefulness.

Reporting Structure

The structure of the reporting system can either enhance or impede the performance of the global account management program. It is important for the success of the global account management program that the personnel involved with the program are not put in a position to choose between meeting the goals of the global account program and the goals of the national or local sales teams. Having the global account program reporting to at least the VP of sales or higher, instead of reporting to country, division, or product managers, the amount of conflict regarding goal attainment is dramatically reduced and the access to appropriate and necessary resources is increased (**Figure 6.1**).

Figure 6.1: Systems and Processes

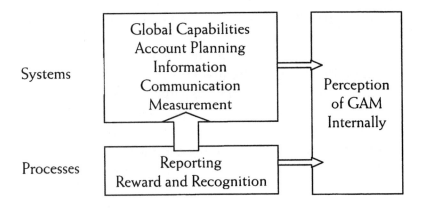

However, just because the global account management program in general reports to the appropriate person or level does not mean that there will not be any conflict. With resource constraints, it is inevitable that there is a degree of dual reporting where local GAM team members and support staff report to both the global account manager and to local field sales or service management. This may cause a dilution of effectiveness unless managed with sensitivity and clarity.

One solution would be to assign all of the people involved only to the global account management program. Yet, as most already know, that situation would drastically increase the cost of the global program and decrease the attractiveness of the program. Spreading personnel out over various programs (due to either time needed or geographic limitations) is a very real issue for many companies.

Another possible solution is to structure the reward and recognition program to include those members that are not totally assigned to the global account management program. By providing compensation (usually in the form of bonuses) for reaching global account goals and recognition (within the company) for their contribution to the success of the global account program, these people are better able to justify their activity and commitment to helping the company focus on the global accounts. It is also important that the less tangible contributions made by local people, not only those associated directly with the creation of sales, are recognized.

Measurement Process
The value of having specific measurements in place is to help management determine if the individual global accounts as well as the global account program are effective and efficient. Without the appropriate measures, it will be difficult for a company to determine anything about each account or the global program. These measures are also useful to see if the resources dedicated to the program and each global account produces the desired results. If the appropriate measures are not in place, then resource decisions

are left to chance. However, embracing and using specific and known measures will aid in the justification and expansion of global account management within the company.

Measurement in most companies seems to revert to dollar or product volume sold as a way to measure success. Even with a simple measure like sales volume, it is still hard to use the information to address other specific issues that are unique to global account management. This simplified view of success as being more than sales is obviously fraught with pitfalls. The global account management process should view the dollar or product sales as a result of specific activities and intermediate goals and not the singular focus (dollar or product sales). In fact, the short-term sales volume focus may be at odds with the long-term growth goals for a customer's business. Sales volume is important to global account management programs, but it should not be the only focus. By introducing other measurement items, the global account team knows what areas to focus on for both short- and long-term success.

Some companies have used some less than scientific measures to measure the global account program. Various U.S. companies have used the measures of customer perception listed below partially or wholly to measure performance effectiveness.

To what extent does the customer believe:

- We are able to provide solutions?
- The sales organization is responsive?
- The support operations are responsive?
- We partner well to provide solutions?
- We are easy to do business with?
- We deliver value?

> *There seems to be a real correlation between the customer's perception of our adding value and our ability to play long-term. This may be a real key indicator.*
>
> Mike Cohen, Hewlett Packard

There are other measurement areas that can be important to consider in global account management programs. A partial list is provided to stimulate thought:

- Obtaining specific objectives for the account (both next year and three years out)
- Identifying what specific actions need to be taken to reach short and long term objectives (along with the blocks to reaching the objectives)
- Tying specific objectives to a time line (milestones)

To assist in obtaining the specific information needed to put together the above objectives, the global team needs to be able to communicate in an effective manner within and outside of the company. This issue will be addressed in the next section. In addition, each of the issues needs to be easily measurable and obtainable by the global team. The idea is to have information available so that the global account manager and team members can identify and prioritize the areas that need attention so that changes can be made. Without a system that captures the appropriate information in a timely manner, the global account manager and team members are in the dark. Thus, global account managers must be able to interface with the IS systems people in order to ensure that the correct measures are being taken to provide information relevant to the global team.

Having the correct measurements being taken by the company ensures that the company is better able to provide appropriate reward and recognition for the global team. Because the sales to global customers involve longer sales cycles, it is important to have other issues to reward and recognize global team members since it may take over a year to accomplish some of the global account goals.

Global account management programs can be more accurately managed, evaluated, and rewarded with the inclusion of the right measures (not just sales volume), such as:

- The development of a process map of the customer
- The development of in-depth relationships with the key contacts
- The identification of new opportunities

Besides improving the planning process, these measures are necessary to the development of an effective reward and recognition system.

Reward and Recognition System

Global Account Manager Pay

Four topics are addressed in this section. One issue is total amount of compensation received by global account managers. The second is the amount of total compensation that comes in the form of incentives. The third area deals with the total pay for global account managers living in different parts of the world and the fourth deals with the use of incentive pay in different parts of the world.

The fact that global account managers require a unique and hard to find set of skills means that the total pay may need to be higher in order to attract and retain them. In a recent study done in the U.S., global account managers were paid on average about 8 percent more than national account managers. Given that the absolute value of the pay may vary by industry, the study did confirm that total compensation for global account managers would be more than for any other selling function.

The same study examined the role of incentive pay for various types of selling functions ranging from telesales to global account management. It found that the relative proportion of incentive pay to basic salary increased from telesales to its apex at the national account management level. The percentage of incentive pay received by global account managers decreased by 3 percent from the level received by national account managers. Thus, the role of incentive pay for a global account manager is less important than for national account managers and senior salespeople. One reason for the higher level of total compensation and lower levels of incentive may be linked to the global account manager position and activities. A global account manager has less direct control over actual sales, and they must function through influence, not direct authority, which means that incentives are much less controllable than with other forms of selling.

Many companies have used team incentives as a way to reward the global team. It was found that 58 percent of global account managers participate in a team incentive program. While that is not an overwhelming endorsement for the practice, it does show that only 42 percent of the U.S. companies studied have not engaged in this practice yet. The most frequent participants in a global team incentive were the national account managers. Over 55 percent of companies that had global team incentives stated that the national account manager was included in the team.

Finally, there is the issue of total pay and incentives paid to global account managers located in different parts of the world. In some parts of the world (though not usually in the U.S.), it would be unheard of for a salesperson to receive more pay than the boss. So, how do companies expect to handle the compensation of global account managers located in different parts of the world? The aforementioned study of U.S. companies found that 58 percent of the companies did, in fact, pay global account managers doing the same job in different parts of the world a different level of pay. That includes both the total and incentive portions. Thus, a majority of U.S. based corporations have learned that what works in America may not work in other parts of the world. They have embraced compensation plans that allow for differences and have not imposed American standards on the rest of the world. However, 42 percent of companies are still professing a "one size fits all" mentality.

The message here is that the compensation plan for global account managers must be designed specifically to meet the needs of the program. Just patching an existing program will only cause problems that will need to be addressed later. The old adage, "prior planning prevents poor performance" can certainly be applied here.

Impact On Others
The topic of reward and recognition is of much interest to not only the global account manager but also the national account manager and the local salesperson. The fact that the global account management program will impact the sales of product and services of both the national account management program and local salespeople means that there is a potential for conflict and discontent for everyone. Historically, country managers, sales people, and national

account managers have been rewarded based on orders generated and/or delivered within geographical boundaries. In relation to global accounts, orders may well be generated from HQ and delivered anywhere in the world. Local salespeople may perceive that wherever the order was placed, they had a major impact upon securing it for the company. The thorny question: who should receive recognition for generating the business?

This question is not often easy to answer, and a number of possible solutions have evolved, with mixed reviews that attempt to provide a solution. The first is the use of double counting sales. That means that for computation of bonuses (via quota attainment), either the local salesperson or the national account manager (depending on the situation) will receive credit for the sales, along with giving credit to the global account manager. This system has an appeal for the personnel involved, since they will get credit no matter who actually sold the product or services. Thus, there is an incentive for national account managers and local salespeople to at least not interfere with or otherwise block the sales process. There is a plus and minus for the company to engage in the practice of double counting. The upsides are that it is quick and easy to do, both parties gain from any sale, and the people involved are, therefore, more satisfied when their pay is not negatively affected. The downside is that it increases the cost of selling. The profitability or profit margins are being squeezed within the company. In an age of increasing price pressure from customers, the increase in the cost of selling with little gain in productivity may not be the wisest choice.

Another compensation mechanism tried by some companies is to have all those involved (local salespeople or national account managers) participate in a team incentive or bonus program. By using a team bonus plan, the company may be better able to match the amount of reward to the level of contribution made by each party. For example, a global account manager is responsible for the sales of products A, B, and C to company Y globally. Company Y has many locations all over the world, and each of these different locations is called on by a local salesperson.

More sophisticated approaches are emerging, particularly the use of 360-degree assessment and the use of balanced score cards that take account of indirect contributions that are made to the sales process and measures of customer satisfaction that reach beyond sales volume.

The Role of Recognition

Motivation of salespeople has primarily been associated with pay, but recognition can also pay dividends for both personnel and the company. The impact on personnel will be discussed here, and the role of recognition on the global account management program will be discussed in the next section.

The recognition that is provided for members of the global account team can come in many forms and on various levels. This section is not designed to provide an exhaustive list but rather to illustrate the impact of recognition on the performance for both the global account manager and various team members.

Communication within a global team provides an opportunity to recognize personnel for their contribution and commitment to the team's goals. This can be accomplished on an informal level and contained within forms of normal communication within the team. For example, a global account manager can acknowledge the efforts and accomplishments of a team member during normal e-mail, written, telephone, videoconference, or faxed communication. This is especially effective when the acknowledgement is related to the topic of the communication. The recognition within the team accomplished two factors: it keeps the recipient engaged and motivated to work hard on the team, and it motivates other team members to put forth more effort so that they can also be recognized within the group. The recognition offers the recipient a measure of prestige and importance within the team.

In addition, the recognition can be more formal and reach a wider audience. An example of this is when the VP of Sales recognizes the efforts and results of the global account team or individual members at a company meeting. The more diverse the meeting attendees are, the more influential the recognition becomes. That is, the recognition received at a company-wide meeting has more power than the same recognition at a divisional, regional, or local meeting. The same is true of written recognition. Acknowledgement appearing in a company wide newsletter is much more powerful than a memo sent to the global team members.

Other forms of recognition can come by establishing awards to recognize global teams or team members. Care must be taken not to have so many awards that they lose their meaning and impact. There is nothing worse than having every global team and every member within those teams receive recognition. On the other hand, having too few awards or recognition categories can have a limiting effect on motivation. This is especially true when one team or one individual is a consistent winner. Finally, the categories for recognition need to be based on the issues that are known to be influential in obtaining company goals in both the short and long run.

Perception of the GAM Program Within the Company
The impact of recognition for the global account program is that its status can be increased within the company. As was seen with the individuals, the more formal the process of recognition and the wider the audience that is made aware of it, the more the global account management program will be seen by others as a key initiative, one that deserves their support and that of others within the organization.

This wider acceptance of the global account management program is important for sustainability. Companies are constantly reallocating resources. Just because the global account program had initial support for resources from other management areas does not mean that they will not pull that support in favor of some of their own initiatives. The more positive recognition and visibility the global account program receives outside of the sales area, the more likely management will continue to support the program. If other managers within the company are not able to see and hear about the successes of the global account program, they are more likely to question spending resources on it.

Summary

The company that is willing to spend the time and energy to make sure that the above issues are addressed will position themselves as a leader in their business category throughout the world. Those companies must make sure that the information collected is appropriate and accurate so that the reporting system using the input (reward and recognition systems) can bring value. The world-class companies will address the perception of the importance of the global account management program in obtaining corporate goals. Companies must continuously monitor and alter the global account selection and selection process as well as provide for a proper planning system to ensure the maximization of both customer value to the company and company value to the customer. In addition, the company must make sure that all the necessary systems are in place to measure the appropriate metrics, which allow for proper reporting and evaluation. The company has a stake in making sure that both information and communication systems are accessible and compatible between the buyer and seller as well as among various locations within the company. Finally, it is important for the company to develop integrated and sophisticated manufacturing and logistical capabilities to ensure that the global customer receives reliable and consistent delivery of the products needed now and new product developments needed for the future, no matter where they are located.

CHAPTER VII

Facing The Challenge

Chapter VII: Facing the Challenge

In This Chapter:

- **The Challenges to GAM**
- **Learning from Failure**
- **Learning from Success**

Introduction

The implementation of GAM programs often requires that major changes be made to the way the organization operates. Changes occur in strategic direction, the allocation of resources, organizational structures, systems, and processes. The whole way in which the company "goes to market" is put under scrutiny and may be called into question. As a consequence, other changes may occur:

- Changes to compensation and reward systems
- Shifts in power and influence patterns within the organization
- Changes in the way resources are allocated

Organizations are inherently conservative. In one sense, they exist in order to create stability and insulate people who work within them from the constantly changing external environment. In these circumstances GAM is essentially about change management and will meet the same degree of resistance that any other major change will meet.

Challenges to the GAM Program

The issues facing companies striving to implement GAM programs have emerged strongly from the work recently done by the SRT research team. One of the major elements identified as necessary for the effective operation of GAM programs is *organizational commitment*. This is both in terms of senior management executive sponsorship and in terms of support from middle managers and support staff operating within all the functional areas that influence the effective realization of the global strategy at local level. Other elements relate to the global capabilities of the global customer and of the supplier in terms of their ability to deliver and receive a global value proposition.

Four factors have been identified that impact at three different levels on the effectiveness of GAM operations. These are *political, organizational, cultural,* and *operational* factors that occur at the level of the buyer organization, the seller organization, and the connecting systems, processes, and people. These are represented in **Figure 7.1** and will provide the focus for this chapter.

Figure 7.1

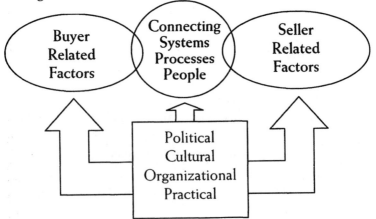

Challenges from the Buyer Organization

The physical capabilities and the psychological (cultural and strategic) readiness on the part of the customer to accept a global offering have a limiting effect on the effectiveness of GAM programs. These factors all impede the buying company's ability to link with the global offering made by the supplier, thereby eliminating the potential benefits.

While the customer purchasing HQ may be able to reach a global agreement, they may have difficulty in implementing that agreement unless their supply chain and procurement management processes are integrated globally. If the customer's operational capabilities lack coordination, much of the value of a global relationship is lost.

Managers at a local level within the customer organization may also favor purchasing from local suppliers, and they may place considerable barriers in the way of an agreement that they perceive as threatening the relationships they have fostered in their own supply markets. They may also perceive the global agreement as a threat to their own authority at local level and resist attempts by HQ to impose the global agreement.

Major problems may also be encountered when the culture of the global customer organization is not supportive of the development of collaborative relationships. Where the global purchasing team is more concerned with wresting the lowest possible global price from their suppliers than with creating long-term value, it is difficult for suppliers to realize the potential for profitability inherent in many global account relationships.

Challenges from the Seller Organization

A major barrier to the operation of GAM programs arises when unresolved conflict exists between the interests of global and local managers. This is easy to understand when we consider the way in which international operations tend to develop.

While in the early stages of internationalization, there tends to be high levels of central control from HQ local managers assuming increasing levels of autonomy as the remote businesses develop in maturity. Local managers take on more authority and control over both day-to-day activities and, often, the strategic direction of regional operations. GAM requires a re-coordination of operations, and local managers often perceive this as a threat to their authority.

The following conditions tend to increase tension between local managers and those attempting to implement the global account management strategy:

- The global vision and strategy has not been effectively communicated throughout the selling organization

- Senior management support is inconsistent

- The global strategy does not recognize local interests and fails to enlist local support

- Compensation issues remain unresolved and are counter-productive to the global strategy

- Existing local power bases are threatened

- Organizational and reporting structures and systems fail to recognize the limitations imposed by organizational complexity and cultural diversity

- Strategies focus largely upon short-term gains in terms of product sales

- The organization lacks a true global outlook

Challenges from Connecting Systems and Processes

There are several factors associated with linking systems and processes that may impede the effective operation of GAM processes.

Lack of Integrated Communications System

GAM is reliant upon the performance of dispersed team members. If these teams are to be managed effectively, there is a strong requirement for communications systems that allow the team members to interact with each other in order to develop, implement, and monitor account strategies regardless of geographical and time differences.

Disjointed Logistical Connections

GAM is dependent upon the same level of service capability being available wherever the customer operates in the world. The ability to deliver the product/service offering within agreed time frames is as important as being able to provide a standardized global product service offering.

Technological Discontinuity

Discontinuities may occur between the supplier's capability to deliver and the customer's ability to receive the global value proposition. Where the supplier displays high levels of technological and process sophistication, their offering may be of limited value to less sophisticated customers. On the other hand, there is an opportunity in these instances for suppliers to help their customers achieve higher levels of sophistication. One example drawn from the textiles industry concerned a supplier of yarn providing its global customer with the process expertise that enabled them to use a new raw material to enhance end-product capabilities. This may also happen in reverse where the global customer "teaches" their suppliers in order to enhance their logistical or process capabilities.

There may be discontinuities *within* both organizations between HQ and remote facilities. Remote operational facilities are often heavily dependent upon local resources to provide infrastructure, personnel, and underpinning technological capabilities. Where there are marked differences between the quality of these inputs in different geographical regions, this is likely to cause problems in terms of global integration and coordination.

There is also a tendency for process variations to evolve at the local level that may have little impact upon manufacturing capability, product quality, and service consistency when applied solely to the local level, but which may have a major impact when viewed from a global perspective. These discontinuities make it difficult to provide a seamless product service offering without investments being made that enhance the capabilities of less able members of the network.

Geographical Non-Alignment of Facilities

Under ideal circumstances the supplier's facilities should mirror those of the customer, but where substantial investment is required, this may not always be possible. The customer may well be of major strategic importance to the supplier, but if there is no additional local demand to warrant the establishment of new facilities, then it may not be economic to make a major new investment. Geographical alignment should be one of the criteria used when identifying and selecting global accounts, and where there is limited fit, serious consideration should be given to extending provision or limiting the nature of the offer made to the global account. Individual decisions should not be taken in isolation, however, and the needs and potential needs of other global customers should be taken into account when deciding upon an expansion of facilities.

Lack of Operational Integration and Coordination

Where the silo effect is very strong, it is virtually impossible to effectively coordinate operations. In companies where decisions relating to operational systems and processes have been taken at local level, there is a strong likelihood that there will be systems incompatibility.

Language and Cultural Differences Not Taken into Account

Cultural colonialism is a major impediment to effective GAM implementation. If the parent company insists on "one best way" of operating without considering strong regional differences in the way in which business is done, there is likely to be strong resistance to the GAM program.

Political Challenges

The adoption of GAM strategies often presents a major challenge to existing organizational structures, established practices, power bases, and lines of authority. As firms internationalize, there is a tendency for control over day-to-day activities, and even some strategic decisions, to devolve from HQ to country or regional managers. The rewards of these managers are often closely tied to the results they obtain in clearly defined geo-

---

What Do Global Account Managers See As Their Major Challenges?

Global/local conflicts of interest=68%

Regional/local implementation of global strategies=61%

Lack of an integrated IT system=50%

Managing and coordinating multi-national teams=44%

Demands of the customer exceed local capability=25%

Language difficulties=24%

Regional/local players damage global relationship=21%

Local capability exceeds global capability=20%

---

graphical areas, and in an attempt to foster higher levels of performance, they are often encouraged to compete with their colleagues from other regions.

The adoption of global strategies requires the reorientation of power, decision-making, and operational coordination towards the center and high levels of cooperation among the different geographical regions and functional areas of the firm. Where local managers perceive that the implementation of global strategies poses a threat to their interests, they are likely, whether overtly or covertly, to resist their implementation. Global/local conflicts of interest are a major impediment to the effective implementation of GAM strategies.

Throughout our research we have seen that a core requirement in overcoming the political barriers to GAM implementation has been the entanglement of senior managers in providing executive sponsorship for the program. Senior executives are often members of a formal team on an Executive Sponsorship Program or Global Steering Committee, or they may provide informal support for the GAM program. Either way, senior executives must ride shotgun, and it is not enough for them to say they support the initiative: they must be seen to support it by their actions.

The essential role of senior executives in their involvement with the GAM program is to facilitate change. They have the political clout to push through the necessary organizational and systems changes, as well as the influence to produce changes in cultural perception and acceptance of the need to embrace the GAM strategy. They also act as internal arbiters assisting with dispute resolution. They have a major role to play in the alignment of internal resources, and can provide access, because of their own contact networks, to higher-level executives within the customer organization. They also have their part to play in helping develop account strategy and in monitoring implementation.

Organizational Challenges

Organizational barriers to GAM implementation include:

- The lack of a clearly defined reporting structure. (**Chapter Five** dealt in some detail with the alternative approaches that may be adopted when striving to deliver the global promise at local level.)
- Poor systems integration and cross-functional coordination.
- Lack of resources.
- "Not invented here" syndrome.
- Poor communication of the global strategy to local personnel.

Clarity in reporting responsibilities is essential. Local people serving the GAM cause must be clear about when they must report to local managers and when global managers demand their attention. There will often be tension between the need to meet the needs of local management and the demands of the global program and care must be taken to define responsibilities and reconcile those differences.

Poor internal systems integration and cross-functional coordination may be the natural result of organizing around regional or country boundaries. The resultant silos tend to develop their own approaches to supply chain management, manufacturing operations, marketing, and internal communications that do not integrate easily with other parts of the organization.

GAM programs are expensive and may not show good returns in the early stages. If they are to succeed, resources in terms of people, money, time, and facilities must be allocated to them. GAM initiatives have to compete, however, with other demands placed upon the company, and without a long-term commitment to the program on behalf of senior managers, factional interests may be successful in staving the program of resources, as we will see illustrated in our first case study below.

Two further barriers are important to address. The first is the tendency of people to resist initiatives that are not their idea, the "not invented here" syndrome. The second is a lack of understanding about the benefits that can be created through serving global customers more effectively. Both need to be addressed through planned and purposeful internal communication of the global strategy and the benefits that accrue, not only to the corporation as a whole but also to local operations that support it. This approach is exemplified in our second case study about the Marriott Corporation.

Cultural Challenges

Culture impacts upon the ability to implement GAM programs at (at least) three levels. First, careful account must be taken of differences in national cultural perspective, and allowances must be made in the way that things are communicated, how people are rewarded, and how business is conducted. What may appear to be the obvious way of doing things from headquarters' perspective may create great problems at a local level. A major barrier to the effective operation of the GAM program is a form of corporate colonialism where HQ, whether based in the U.S., Europe, or the Far East, insists that their way of doing things is the only way to do things. In a complex organizational and cultural environment, it is good to remember that culture represents the way people solve problems and that great sensitivity and tolerance is needed to understand the different approaches that might be adopted by different people to different situations. If the ends are achieved (and no laws are broken), local GAM team members should be empowered to find their own way to salvation (i.e., delivering the global promise).

Second, the company's culture, exhibiting a generally adversarial attitude towards customers and suppliers or focused upon short-term goals and the fostering of national and regional prejudice, may narrow its global vision. It is not impossible to deal at a global level with companies that do not value long-term close relationships, but it is certainly more difficult. Many companies seek global partners that exhibit similar views of the world and have similar strategic objectives. Those customers should always provide the main focus for resource allocation, but it also needs to be recognized that some global customers, while not offering the same potential for partnership and joint value creation, must nevertheless be managed, if only because they represent such a large opportunity for volume business. The critical observation is that not all relationships, even those with global customers, are necessarily close but all require to be managed for profitability.

A third area of cultural dissonance occurs between the different functional specialties within organizations. Sales people and marketers tend to adopt different cultural perspectives from those of manufacturing engineers, accountants, and purchasing people. Many of these differences are not purely cultural and may reflect the way they are rewarded, the way they were trained, and the roles they perform. Nevertheless, when constructing global teams, when communicating, and when setting targets and objectives, these differences must be taken into account.

Practical Challenges

We have observed practical difficulties experienced when determining and operationalizing global pricing policies, meeting different national and regional specifications and regulations, allocating resources to account development, and developing internal agreement to make the necessary adaptations for global account management. Difficulties in collecting, collating, and disseminating information, and in sustaining the global network of customer relationships, were other problems highlighted.

Responses to the Challenges that Face GAM Programs

Different companies respond differently to the challenges faced by GAM programs. Their response is partly a reflection of the core cultural values embodied in the company, and partly a reflection of executive capability to manage the politically charged environment within which GAM operates and to create innovative ways of meeting the needs of both internal and external customers.

Whatever Happened to GAM?

In the previous chapter, we summarized the case of a Midwestern U.S. company that closed down its GAM operation in the face of increasing internal opposition to the GAM project. Here we present the case in full because it provides a salutary lesson in the power of internal politics and the lack of real senior management commitment to the program to destroy the GAM initiative.

Case 1: Push-Pull Co. Inc

The Background to the GAM Project

Push-Pull is a market leader in its field and over the years has carved a truly enviable market share within the U.S. The imaginative name for the firm had come about because of the technology they employed to make materials handling equipment. Push-Pull produce systems that are capable of moving a variety of materials through pipes and ductwork by applying pressure or suction. The systems are sold into a variety of industrial markets including power generation, for transporting fuel from hoppers to furnaces; the food industry, for the movement of ingredients from storage to mixing and packaging facilities; the pharmaceutical and chemicals industries; and wherever materials handling requires closed systems.

The world HQ is based in the U.S. in the parent company offices. Early ventures by export sales people led to the establishment of manufacturing facilities in the U.K., Germany, and two facilities in the Far East. Over the years, this expanded to a worldwide presence with affiliates in 25 countries providing sales and customer support to Fortune 500 companies as well as national firms.

Push-Pull was organized into two divisions, Domestic Sales (U.S.) and International. There had always been an intense rivalry between these two groups, spurred on by sales incentive credits, turf divisions, and responsibilities. The network of affiliates had enjoyed what the company called *autonomous jurisdiction*. This freedom on the part of affiliates to act independently was a cornerstone of the company's philosophy, but in recent years this broad-based network of distribution was increasingly perceived as a barrier to Push-Pull becoming a truly global company. The potential for increasing the company's market share in the U.S. was seen as limited, and for some years the company had recognized that it must look overseas for real growth potential.

Push-Pull had had a National Accounts program for over 20 years that promoted special pricing for large domestic accounts. They still maintain a national sales force that calls on end user accounts, promotes the products and systems, and provides technical advice to the distributor network.

The GAM Program

In response to these factors, Bill Craymer was appointed from within the company as VP Global Accounts in order to spearhead the global initiative. Bill had served the company for over ten years, first as a field sales engineer, then variously as an area sales manager and NAM (national accounts manager), and then as Director of National Accounts. Bill had been a major advocate for the adoption of a GAM strategy. When first appointed as the GAM for the company, he had some ideas, initially not clearly formed, about the development and maintenance of a Global Account program:

- He knew his firm had a global manufacturing and distribution capability and believed that this strength could be parlayed into a program that would deliver higher value to customers and give it the advantage over the competition.
- He knew that this capability needed to be coordinated worldwide.

- He had five years NAM experience and therefore had a general idea of the direction he should take in terms of developing customer relationships.

- He had the support of senior management.

- He was aware that culture might play a pretty big part in helping or hindering the achievement of his goals. The corporate culture within the company encouraged competition between affiliates to produce better results than their "rivals". As the world market place began to shrink and competition increased, management had begun to see that this segmented sales effort was having a detrimental effect upon their relationships with customers. Nevertheless, old habits die hard, and people were slow to see the advantages of collaborating with other divisions within the company.

- Turf wars abounded in the organization, and he knew that there was an urgent need to put together a team for the development process.

- Even though he had the support of the CEO, he knew that not everyone, even at HQ, would be supporting his efforts.

- He was not sure which customers should be approached, or even what to approach them with.

- He was also aware that he would need an effective method of gathering and monitoring information and that he would need to establish some sort of global organization to implement the program.

Bill had begun the process by recruiting a number of highly committed people to his team, drawn from the domestic sales organization. They had spent time beginning the global account development program by identifying those multi-national accounts that were located in the U.S. The majority of these accounts were former national accounts. Selection criteria were established based upon historical sales data and information from the sales organization. Push-Pull's top 100 accounts were singled out, and sales managers were assigned to enhance relationships and develop global sales opportunities.

There were some problems with implementing this strategy because there had been a recent switch from direct sales to alternate channels of distribution in the U.S., using distributors. The idea of working with U.S. based accounts had been to uncover business opportunities with their foreign operations. With the change in channel design there was now a need to enlist the support of those distributors with international capabilities and work through them.

Some of those distributors saw the opportunity this offered to increase their business. However, it was difficult to reconcile their needs with those of the foreign affiliates, in whose territory they would have to operate in order to deliver a global capability to those customers who were part of the program.

There were some initial successes. A number of opportunities were uncovered by the Domestic Sales Division and passed on to the International Division. What was still lacking, however, was an account responsibility structure that transcended divisional boundaries. Bill realized that until a more coordinated global account management system was established, with a comprehensive communications system and an integrated strategy supported by the whole organization, Push-Pull would not reap the rewards.

Meanwhile, behind the scenes and largely unknown to Bill, opposition was growing. Divisional managers who complained that they were losing business and that existing relationships were being endangered by the new global initiative were lobbying the CEO. Some people also pointed out the cost and the lack of tangible results during the months it had been in operation. Things came to a head when one of the most powerful affiliates complained that a major contract had been lost to a U.S. distributor. If this was how the program was going to operate, they wanted no part of it.

Under considerable pressure from a number of sources, the CEO reached the decision that the risks associated with continuing with the GAM project outweighed the benefits that could be realized in the foreseeable future. He called Bill in to give him the bad news that the program was to be terminated and the GAM team members were to be reassigned to other duties.

What Went Wrong?

This case is based upon a real situation. The name of the company has been changed, as has the industry that it operates in, but the issues and the broad sequence of events that are related here reflect what actually happened over the past year. The case is interesting because it reflects the approach adopted by many companies new to the idea of global account management.

There was a basic misunderstanding of this relatively new phenomenon. Adopting GAM processes is not a quick fix. Implementing GAM strategies takes time. Some companies reckon that payback can take a minimum of three to four years and sometimes longer. Push-Pull expected results in months, not years.

During the time that GAM processes are evolving within a company, everything is up for review. Existing structures, power bases, systems, processes, the very business that you believe you are in, will need to be questioned. Serving customers at a global level will have a fundamental impact upon your business, and if you are not prepared to change, do not embark on the process, because it is doomed to failure. Push-Pull tried to overlay GAM processes, which are essentially concerned with coordinating effort, onto a system that was inherently divisive. Senior management lacked the will, as well as the vision, to challenge the old ways of doing things.

There was a lack of clarity about what characterized a global customer and what was a realistic number of customers that could be served globally. Even the largest companies begin their GAM programs by identifying only a handful of customers that they could classify as truly global, and of those, most chose only one or two with whom they felt a global relationship could be developed. Was it realistic for Push-Pull to expect to start by developing 100 global customers?

Meeting the Challenges of the GAM Program

A major factor in overcoming some of the challenges to the GAM program is effective internal promotion. In many GAM programs we explored, frequent and organization-wide communication of progress and success stories was cited as vital to sustaining the effort. In addition, executive support needed active maintenance, and the GAM process needed to be ingrained into organizational routines, systems, and processes. None of this can happen overnight. Recognition that **GAM is a long-term process** has been identified across our research as a major message to emerge from the experience of respondents.

Valuable insights into how one company has addressed these challenges are to be found in the experiences of Marriott International in developing their Alliance Account Program. The following case is drawn from a recent article published in the *Journal of Selling and Major Account Management* and is reprinted by kind permission of the SRT. It reports on a conversation between Steve Richard of Marriott and an SRT researcher.

Case 2: The Marriott Experience

Marriott International provides interesting insights into how one company addressed some of these problems, in particular how they developed organization-wide commitment to the *Global Alliance Program*. The Marriott Corporation has grown into one of the world's major hotel groups, operating 1700 locations worldwide. While the GAM Study highlighted the challenge facing all organizations attempting to facilitate the local implementation of global strategies, these are of particular significance at Marriott because the majority of their hotels are owned, not by them directly, but by independent franchisees.

How the Alliance Program Started at Marriott

The Alliance Program began with the realization at the most senior levels within the organization that customers were demanding more from Marriott than just hotel rooms, and that Marriott was capable of delivering much more in terms of real value to their major customers. A strategic decision was taken to reorganize the entire sales enterprise within Marriott, building upon three key initiatives:

1. Develop the technology to support connectivity
2. Refocus the sales force personnel on markets rather than individual hotels
3. Develop a global account management program

While major customers had been asking for a single point of contact for some time, their vision of what that single point of contact could do was different from Marriott's. Initially customers view *single contact* as a tactical solution to their pricing problems, whereas Marriott took a much more holistic approach and perceived the single contact as a single *con-*

sultant contact with the potential to address issues of major strategic importance to both the customer and themselves.

Internal Challenges in Implementing the Program

First there was the problem of moving a traditional, primarily transactional, sales organization toward a more total account solutions focused one. This move was not intended to ignore the needs of individual customers—the right level of service to meet their needs still needed to be allocated—but there was recognition that certain high-valued external assets (e.g., alliance accounts) require an enterprise-to-enterprise approach.

When Marriott began making the change from local, to cluster, to market, to regional, to national, to a global focus for the sales operation, the perceived loss of control over sales influence by the local hotel management team proved unsettling. Previously they had control from budget to strategy on which customers their sales team targeted. They are now part of a larger organization.

Part of that larger organization is the GAM program, which is not concerned with filling rooms at one hotel but, rather, takes a broader view, and that involves assuming control and responsibility for those accounts completely. The local sales team is giving up some of their power and autonomy. This is difficult, and transition can be stressful. However, they do retain total control because they retain the ability to price and yield the product.

The second major challenge was the sheer size of the task of communicating across the enterprise. Even if everyone agreed to make the necessary changes immediately, that still left the problem of communicating with 130,000 associates within the entire company, and even if you limit it to the salespeople, that still leaves 5-6000 associates.

When you have that many people involved, there will always be those for whom this type of change is seen as just another initiative "de jour." If they do not openly oppose it and do not really support it, maybe it will just die a slow death, and they can go back to doing it the old way. This is not uncommon behavior.

A third problem was measurement. With so many people involved, it was very difficult to agree on what was the new standard of measurement for the GAM. How should resources and rewards be allocated, and over what period should people be measured?

External Challenges in Implementing the Program

One major problem was to get customers to think beyond price and to change their perception about what it means to be an Alliance Account. Often the customer thinks that they have finished with the process, while the Marriott team feels they are only just beginning. The customer is happy with a central point of contact and some sort of pricing agreement, while Marriott wants to "ratchet up" the relationship to go across their enterprise and figure out ways to begin creating value that is recognizable. That's a big issue.

A second issue is the customer purchasing personnel's willingness or ability to get comfortable with Marriott being given access throughout their organization. The Marriott vision is to act as a professional consultant who is leveraging the enterprise to find and generate solutions and value. While almost all customers want additional value, arriving at what that value really is and what form it takes is a wide-open field. Often their vision is for Marriott to respond to their direction and vision with product, service, price, and advice. Buyers are also afraid that by giving us access to their organization, they may be made less valuable. However, the opposite is true—we want to make them more valuable.

How Marriott Changed Customer Perceptions

> *I finished a meeting two days ago up in New York with IBM where, at the end of the meeting, they said to me, 'You are now the only supplier that we are going to deal with when piloting anything new. Everyone else, the Hiltons, the Starwoods, and the other people, will be the follow-up people who will get it after you, and I have piloted everything.' That's the accumulation of one year's worth of work on my relationship with IBM since the early days when they were only interested in our solving pricing problems for them.*
>
> Steve Richard, Marriott International

The first requirement, in Steve Richard's opinion, is that you must flawlessly execute the customer's baseline expectation before you can make them move on from thinking, "One point of contact will help me with my pricing issues." Once that is achieved and a small number of successes have been delivered to the client, the buyer begins to feel more comfortable with you and your approach and organization, and you can begin to lead him towards the Promised Land. By helping them with small successes, you can begin to build the relationship.

Innovation: The Key to GAM Success

Much of the success that Marriott has enjoyed with the Alliance Account Program is due to the innovative approach they take to defining and resolving customer problems. Below are two examples of the way in which the relationship with one of Marriott's most important Global Alliance Accounts, IBM, has been enhanced through the development of innovative approaches to the GAM process.

> *Well, we look at things that may appear pretty mundane but actually get at the heart of how we will do business together in the future. Last year IBM paid us over $2,000,000 in cancellation fees for meeting rooms. They paid us another $15,000,000 for meeting rooms they actually*

used. So, they're paying over 10 percent of their budget for meetings in cancellation fees; that's a huge proportion. The idea we're going to be piloting involves setting up an internal, that's internal to Marriott and IBM, electronic bulletin board where any meetings that get cancelled would immediately be put on this electronic bulletin board and sold to other IBM customers. If the cancelled meeting space is filled by another IBM opportunity, the cancellation fee will no longer apply. Instead of paying the full cancellation fee, the original meeting customer would only be liable for the difference. Everybody wins. We're happy because someone shows up to use the space, the original booker saves most or all of his cancellation charge, and the new booker gets what they need at a potentially lower cost. If there is a difference in the revenue from the original booking, that difference is settled within IBM.

Electronic purchase orders, bill submissions, and electronic payments are also in the works. Electronic transmission of individual traveler folio data directly into their global expense management system is now a reality. These initiatives get to the heart of their strategic initiative to move into a total B2B environment. Two months ago I was traveling in Europe with one of my customers, with the aim of helping to figure out how they redesign their non-U.S. strategy on consolidation of accommodation expenditure. As the relationship developed, the focus has become increasingly strategic. My role has effectively changed from being a consultant on price to helping to resolve business problems to being an organizational-issue consultant. Not only does trust grow during this time, but the impact of problems also diminishes and a tolerance for mundane issues increases—they become minor irritations instead of decision-making factors.

Steve Richard, Marriott International

The Impact of Communication on Internal Challenges

This kind of innovative approach to the management of global customer relationships has a major impact upon removing the internal barriers to GAM implementation. Demonstrations of success breed understanding within the company of the value of the program. Value needs to be demonstrated so frequently that it acts to overcome the inertia and the concerns of the people who may provide barriers to implementation.

The core issue is one of internal communication, and Marriott has spent a great deal of time evolving not only account development plans, but also internal marketing plans. A strategy has been devised that identifies multiple audiences throughout the enterprise who are critical to the success of the global alliance program. By constant communication, the aim is to either gain their support or give them enough information to continue to help them better understand the advantages of the overall global alliance program strategy.

Having identified those internal markets, people are assigned to continually address them in order to gain their support. The GAM Vice President engages Marriott's senior executives on a daily basis with information on customers, the market environment, competitive information, and successes. The regional global account managers engage all of the key decision-makers in their part of the world, from SVP on down to cluster directors, by being involved in their local organizations (i.e., being on the agendas for their meetings, continually communicating, etc.)

Senior members of the Global Alliance Program regularly present the GAM story and strategy at the Director of Marketing Forum. Every few months all the new directors of marketing from across the world are gathered together for school. People like Steve Richard go and present the mission, vision, and game plan to them and make sure they understand exactly who is involved in the program and what they do and the value to them. The aim is to have speakers from the program on the agenda of every meeting throughout the organization, from general manager annual meetings to local sales force, marketing, or even finance meetings.

Address the Needs of Those Who Present the Challenges
Quite apart from achieving success with customers and communicating those successes throughout the organization, members of the team also recognize the importance of addressing and meeting the needs of their internal markets.

The local facility management teams are primarily concerned with the business they generate locally, rather than with the needs of global companies that may or may not contribute to their business objectives. However, they are interested in gaining business from the global account; they are also interested in information about their competitors, and the Global Alliance is well placed to help them achieve both those objectives. They may want better access to the account's decision-makers in their own territories, and very often the global team can facilitate that, as well as assisting with the establishment of account pricing and development strategies and ongoing account marketing issues. Just as the global account manager acts as consultant to the external customer, so they also play the role of consultant to the internal customer. The internal strategy designed to meet the challenge posed by resistance to the program in fact mirrors the external strategy in the way it addresses the strategic business needs of internal "customers" in order to alter their perception of the value of the GAM program.

At one level the local hotel receives protection from the negative impact that dynamic market conditions may have on the external customer. If the global alliance team has done a good job of developing a robust relationship with the global customer, that provides insulation against downturns in the marketplace. Marriott's share of business doesn't go down when the pie gets smaller, and that can translate all the way to the local market because they see their competitors' business go down at a much more accelerated rate than theirs. Defending against erosion or downturn is perceived as just as critical as driving new revenues.

At a more significant level, the global relationship creates new opportunities for local salespeople, giving them access to key decision-makers. A whole range of other non-financial values is created in just the same way as non-financial values are created for external customers. By being involved in the process, local players get a sense that they are part of it, that they have some control, that they have some contribution.

One of the more tangible benefits available to local sales teams is that the global customer review process developed for the alliance program can be used to listen to local customers to identify their key drivers. The cost of analysis and report writing for this exercise is absorbed under the global alliance budget. Thus, at no cost to their own facility, the local sales person is transformed in the eyes of the local buyer into a mini-consultant with the ability to listen to their issues and come up with solutions. This has the effect of immediately differentiating them from their local competition.

Key Learning Points

The Marriott experience provides some valuable insights into how to overcome organizational barriers to the implementation of global account strategies. What the Global Alliance Account Team has identified is that a clear and cohesive strategy needs to be developed to promote the program *inside* the organization in similar ways to the strategies developed for external customers:

- Selling the idea of the GAM program in-house is as important as selling the idea to customers.

- The internal sales process should be linked to the broader GAM strategies and stress the value that it delivers, not just in broad organizational terms, but also in local and individual ways.

- The way to change internal customer perception is to build on small rapid successes that address important issues for the key players within the organization. In addressing internal blocks to the implementation of the GAM process, the Marriott Team has identified that they reflect many of the concerns of external customers and can often be resolved by applying similar solutions.

Critical Elements of the Program

Recognizing the Challenge: Meeting the challenge of overcoming organizational resistance to the Global Alliance program involved a recognition that legitimate concerns might exist among senior corporate and local managers, franchisees, and the sales force. There was also a willingness to address those concerns by identifying and delivering the value inherent in the program, not just to the organization as a whole, but to the individuals within it who would be instrumental, through their actions, in ensuring its success or failure.

Planning: The second element of the process is planning. As much care and attention to detail was paid to developing internal sales strategies as to those developed for the Alliance Accounts. People within the Alliance Team were charged with the responsibility of selling the idea to all levels of the organization and in all locations. Everyone was involved.

Communication: The core of the program was, and still is, communication: communicating the process, benefits, and successes throughout the organization. Formal presentations are made at all levels of management and at corporate and local facilities. Communication is also informal and constant ensuring that people are kept in the loop and made to feel involved in the process.

Networking: Just as attempts are made to network within the Alliance Account, so networking has been recognized as of great importance within Marriott.

Identifying Customer Need: Not only were the concerns of internal customers recognized, but their specific needs were, also. These were addressed at a business level in terms of protecting or developing revenue, at an organizational level in terms of delivering training and staff development opportunities, and at a strategic level. For example, this was achieved at an individual level by providing sales staff with the tools to turn them into local business consultants to their clients, and at higher levels by providing opportunities for local hotels to grow their business with *their* key strategic accounts.

Organizational Change: Marriott has recognized that organizational change, in terms of changing the focus of the sales force activity away from serving the needs of particular hotels towards a greater focus upon customers, is a long-term requirement. This change is ongoing and recognizes the need to act sensitively towards local managers who may still not be fully convinced of the benefits that the alliance program will deliver.

Delivering: The final part of the process involves ensuring, as with external customers, that the promised benefits are delivered.

Summary

GAM programs face a number of challenges both from the external environment and from within their own organizations. If those challenges are to be met effectively, care must be taken to select global account managers with sufficient business acumen and political/cultural sensitivity to negotiate the minefield of complex issues they face. They must be allocated resources in terms of people, time, and finance to carry out their work and be provided with the ongoing support and entanglement of senior executives who are aware of the difficulties but committed to the potential of the program.

CHAPTER VIII

Sustaining The Effort

Chapter VIII: Sustaining the Effort

Introduction

In the last chapter we explored some of the barriers to GAM operations. In this chapter we will discuss the approaches that have been adopted by companies in sustaining the GAM initiative. Three elements are identified as being important in this respect: the strategic elements of global account management, operational issues, and infrastructure issues.

Strategic issues are concerned with the classification and identification of global accounts with approaches to account planning and with the role of the global account manager. The operational issues that we shall explore include the global structures, systems, and processes that global suppliers adopt. The infrastructure elements of GAM programs address process management, reporting systems, and knowledge management issues.

Successful GAM programs display the following attributes:

- They are developed at corporate level and enjoy executive sponsorship
- The duties of the global account manager and the GAM team have been clearly delineated
- There is a clearly defined account selection process
- They have an electronically supported Account Planning Process
- There is customer involvement in the process
- They have a strong supporting infrastructure

Components of Success

Strategic Components

The single most important contribution to the continued success of the GAM program is the presence of sustained corporate level sponsorship. This entanglement of senior managers at a strategic level goes beyond bringing the program to fruition, to ensuring its sustainability through the provision of resources and demonstrations of their continuing support.

A further strategic imperative is the need to establish clear criteria and processes by which new global account customers are identified and chosen. This process goes beyond the identification of individual customers that was discussed in Chapter Three to embrace the concept of developing a portfolio of global accounts segmented based on their attractiveness to the supplier and the potential they hold for developing a global value creating relationship.

Resources in even the largest organization are limited, and the process of developing global relationships is necessarily expensive. There is no shortage of customers demanding a global value proposition, but some are more attractive than others. For these reasons it is important that the choice of global customer is given careful consideration. While to many suppliers the choice of global customer at first seems obvious, "Surely they are those that represent the largest potential for increasing business volume," those with longer experience of managing global accounts realize that other factors are equally, if not more, important:

- Operational capability to receive the global offering
- Strategic synergy

- Cultural affinity
- The value placed upon buyer-seller relationships in general and the specific relationship in particular
- Willingness to invest in the relationship for mutual benefit
- The specific needs the customer and the fit between the core competencies of both organizations

It is important that the question of selection is removed from the political arena of the organization. If the choice of global customers is left to the whim of individuals, they are likely to make the choice on irrational grounds, or on the basis that they have particular importance to the individuals concerned, be they local or corporate managers. A further danger is that of post-selection rationalization. If no process exists to guide relational choice, the likelihood is that sound reasons will be identified after the event to justify the decision. These approaches will inevitably lead to sub-optimal relational performance.

Clear guidelines need to be established before individual customers are discussed and before decisions are made as to how well they fit the template that is developed from the weighted criteria that have been objectively established.

The process of selection will result in the differentiation of customers into different categories based on their attractiveness and their potential for relational development. Category one global customers will be those of supreme strategic importance and potential, while those of lesser importance and potential will make up second, third, and perhaps fourth tier categories. Categorization in this fashion allows for the allocation of scarce resources to those accounts that will generate the greatest return on investment.

While at present we observe that in many industries only a few suppliers have the potential to achieve "first mover" advantage by providing a truly global value proposition to clients, competitor capability is increasing. It is important, therefore, to develop the ability to manage not only those relationships with the most important global customers, but also those with lesser potential, albeit at lower cost.

Effective strategy setting for each account is a trademark of successful GAM. This requires that planning processes are in place which are designed to capture important information upon which to base decisions, and that involves all members of the team in strategy formulation, implementation, and review. These issues will be given further attention later in this chapter. What is important here is that consideration is given to the level within the organization at which the global account manager is appointed, and what the relationship is between the GAM account leader and the rest of the team.

The companies that have been most successful in implementing and sustaining GAM programs are those that signal the importance of the global account manager role by having them report high up in their organization and have defined the reporting responsibilities of team members, providing a clear mandate for them to perform their global responsibilities.

The final strategic issue is the choice of global account manager and the members of the GAM team. The global account manager is key to the success of the GAM program, and his or her talents provide the focus for discussion later in this chapter.

Operational Components

Structural issues were discussed in some detail in Chapter Five. Systems and processes associated with successful

GAM may be viewed as following a number of stages, evident in the "Twelve Steps to Success" applied by a leading world-class financial services company in their global customer management program:

1. Align the management team and mobilize for action (enlist senior executive support)
2. Assess the supplier organization's readiness for change (identify core global competencies)
3. Segment clients (identification and classification)
4. Profile clients (determine level of attractiveness and potential for exploitation)
5. Listen to clients to identify their strategic imperatives (establish core strategic need)
6. Analyze the gaps between present provision and the potential for growing the business (confirm attractiveness)
7. Mobilize the global account team (fit team capabilities to customer need)
8. Outline the strategic action program (develop strategic focus)
9. Validate and assess the fit of the action plan (seek customer confirmation)
10. Engage core teams, projects teams and issue teams (to operate at different levels and degrees of closeness with the customer to implement the plans)
11. Implement strategies and activities
12. Track performance

At an operational level, these processes are concerned with issue management, the management of relationships in order to enhance the customer perception of the supplier's brand value, and with managing the account team.

Infrastructure Components

Infrastructure issues are broadly concerned with managing the process, with ensuring effective reporting structures, and with knowledge management. Effectiveness in these areas is associated with a number of elements being in place:

- Training and education of global account managers and global team members
- Compensation systems
- Communications processes
- Measurement systems to gauge customer satisfaction
- Account planning and support technology
- Global pricing and contract methodology

Global Capabilities

Underpinning the components of GAM success are a number of global competencies in terms of product development, manufacturing and supply, information management, account planning, and management capabilities.

Global markets provide opportunities for product and service extension and adaptation. Two imperatives emerge from this potential. The first is that companies must look beyond their present base product or service offering and seek opportunities for applying their own core competencies to create new orders of value for their customers. At first sight, these may appear to have little in common with the products and services they have traditionally offered. For example, in the case of Marriott cited in the previous chapter, how does the application of technological capabilities in order to solve budgetary management problems for their global customers relate to their core business of providing hotel accommodation? Second, they must look beyond their individual core competencies to identify the potential for building synergistic value by combining their competencies with those of their customers. It is increasingly important that suppliers collaborate, not only to develop new products and services with their customers, but also to effect the adaptation of existing offerings to conform to global/local requirements.

The provision of a seamless global value proposition is dependent upon the coordination of manufacturing, purchasing, transportation, warehousing, and information management processes involved in acquiring, producing, and moving goods and services to wherever in the world the customer operates and requires them. Not only must the global supplier be adept at managing their own processes in this area, but they must also be capable of collaborating and coordinating with customers as well as with their own suppliers and intermediaries in the marketplace. How these competencies are applied will depend upon the strategic focus adopted by the global team.

Strategic Approaches to GAM

Three contrasting but hierarchical strategic approaches to global account management may be discerned. One we have called *Economic GAM*, the second, *Innovative GAM*, and the third, *Entrepreneurial GAM*. Each is a valid approach to managing global customer relationships, depending upon the potential of the global customer for relational development and value creation.

Economic GAM

An economic approach to GAM focuses upon cost reduction and profit enhancement activities that are aimed at increasing sales volume and supply chain efficiencies. This is an approach that we see when customers are focused upon achieving global economies of scope and scale, without interest in developing the closer relationships with their suppliers that could enhance mutual benefit. The task for the supplier in such cases is to reduce cost of serving while gaining access to the potentials for increased product or service sales and share-of-wallet.

Innovative GAM

Innovative GAM programs were evidenced by a high degree of collaboration across the design chain. Indeed, 31 percent of our study conducted their design and development processes on a global, coordinated, and collaborative basis. Such GAM programs were associated with rapid technological change both in terms of product technology and in terms of process and delivery technology. Within such programs, core competencies relate to technical expertise, design project management, and a problem-solving culture. Innovative GAM programs are naturally associated with high-tech industries, but this is not an exclusive relationship, for we observed evidence of design chain activity across a wide range of engineering and service industries. The distinctive factor here is the problem-focused nature of the value-oriented strategies organizations were adopting in order to further their involvement with their global account. The primary innovation we identified related to new ways of augmenting the global offering—either through tailoring products and services to the customer, or through the provision of additional products and services.

Entrepreneurial GAM

Companies adopting an entrepreneurial strategy to drive their global account management processes focus upon the value creation and wider business opportunities inherent in the relationship. They seek ways of integrating their own core competencies and those of their customers in order to achieve synergistic benefits that in some cases result in new business ventures emerging from the relationship.

Which of these approaches is adopted depends upon a number of factors, including the strategic relationship focus adopted by both buyer and seller, and the core competencies of both parties. Where the seller has the competence to deliver each approach, the strategic question is how to structure the account development plan to move the potentially most valuable customers from economic, through innovative, to a realization of the potential value inherent in participating in entrepreneurial GAM. The orchestrator of this process is the global account manager.

The Global Account Manager

Key to the effective implementation and maintenance of GAM processes is the global account manager. We have suggested that GAM is in some respects an extension of national account management, and it is not surprising, then, that many global account managers are drawn from a sales background. In some firms, the position of global account manager is viewed as a proving ground for highly technically qualified general managers being groomed for "higher office." Although selling skills are an important component of the global account manager role, we believe that its performance depends much more upon broader managerial capabilities. We identified three main classes of global account manager competencies relating to analytical skills, levels of international awareness and experience, and a broader set of business and commercial skills that may be classed as entrepreneurial or strategic in nature.

The top ten GAM competencies identified through the research are:

1. Communications skills
2. Global team leadership and management skills
3. Business and financial acumen
4. Relationship management skills
5. Strategic vision and planning capabilities
6. Problem solving capabilities
7. Cultural empathy
8. Selling skills (internal and external)
9. Industry and market knowledge (self and customer)
10. Product/service knowledge

The Political Entrepreneur

Global account management processes rely upon the continued support of senior managers and the complex skills of global account managers. Global account managers, although they must display high levels of selling and persuasive skills, are not primarily salespeople. They are highly skilled relationship managers who can motivate not only the customer, but also people within their own organization to deliver a consistent offering to customers wherever they operate in the world. They must have the ability to communicate effectively in order to build teams; be able to coordinate the activities of others, often with no line authority; and be adept at problem solving.

thority; and be adept at problem solving.

The term that has been coined to describe them is that of *political entrepreneur*. This term captures the essence of the job they perform. They must be adept at treading the corridors of power. They must know the people to speak to, the buttons to press, and the strings to pull, both in their own organization and in the customer's. They must have developed high levels of trust among the people they work with. All these may be seen as political characteristics.

They are essentially concerned with identifying and exploiting opportunity, with solving problems that add value to the relationship, and with innovation in its broadest sense. All these may be seen as entrepreneurial characteristics.

In performing the role of political entrepreneur, the global account manager fulfills a number of important functions:

- Boundary spanning coordinator
- Entrepreneurial strategist
- Team manager/leader
- Politician
- Information broker
- Relationship facilitator/builder
- Negotiator

Many other positions carry boundary-spanning responsibilities. What makes the boundary-spanning role of the global account manager distinctive is the cultural diversity and organizational complexity that surrounds his/her role. In managing the boundary-spanning role, the global account manager must not only deal with cross-cultural differences in the way people do business, but also with global/local differences in perception about the importance of individual relationships and the perceived value of the GAM initiative. In addition to spanning the boundaries between supplier and customer, the global account manager coordinates the interfaces among different parts of the supplier organization.

As entrepreneurial strategist, the global account manager is concerned with identifying potentials for creating entrepreneurial value. The entrepreneur has been described as a person who can recognize and realize the potential for value creation not immediately obvious to others, someone who is essentially an innovator and visionary—"A dreamer who does." Not all of those who are called global account or relationship managers exhibited this skill, but certainly the most successful did.

The raw materials that the political entrepreneur employs to create value are the capabilities inherent in both the GAM and the buying team, and the underpinning core competencies of both organizations. At an operational level, the joint capabilities of the buyer-seller team are used to create enhanced value through process innovation, changing the way things are done to create savings in the supply chain or through product, systems, or process adaptations. At a strategic level, it is the core competencies of both organizations that are used to create value of quite a different order. Here the result can be the development of totally different ways of doing business, or even the development of new businesses.

As politician, the global account manager is both arbiter and manipulator. It is certainly part of the task to reconcile the often-conflicting interests of customer and supplier, global/local operations and managers, and different functional and factional interests. At the same time, achieving the aims of the global strategy may require a degree of covert activity to develop support for the program without allowing potential opponents time to mount an attack.

Political and entrepreneurial skills are also employed in the other subsidiary roles of leadership, information broker, relationship manager/builder, and negotiator. While global account managers are required display high levels of skill in all those areas, they are little different in nature from similar roles played by other managers, albeit with the added levels of complexity imposed by cultural, geographical, and temporal distance.

Training and Development
Finding people with the necessary skills to be effective global account managers is difficult. Not only does it require a broad and complex set of skills, but also a range of personal characteristics that may be hard to find in one person.

Quite apart from the skills we listed earlier in this chapter, global account managers must be:

- Politically astute
- Entrepreneurial
- Flexible
- Tolerant of ambiguity
- Culturally aware
- Innovative

You may be forgiven for thinking that the only potential candidates must also walk on water, but they do exist and it is our belief that they can also be developed with the right training.

Most global account managers are drawn from within their own organizations, very often promoted from senior sales management or national account management positions. People promoted from within the organization have the advantage that they are familiar with the organization, are likely to have an intimate knowledge of products and people, and are likely to have existing networks of relationships and knowledge of the way things are done. That they are often drawn from a sales background may be less valuable. Selling skills are no doubt important, but more valuable are an intimate knowledge of the internal working of the organization; an understanding of operational, logistical, and supply chain issues; and the ability to create innovative solutions to business problems. It may be that people from a broader general management background provide better material for the role of global account manager than people drawn exclusively from sales. Whatever their background, it is unlikely that global account managers will not benefit from development programs that aim to enhance their skills and capabilities.

From recent work carried out with members of SAMA to determine the training and development needs of global account managers, we suggest there are a number of critical areas that should be addressed by companies developing their own global account manager development programs.

We group the development needs of global account managers under three broad headings: analytical skills, cultural awareness, and business/commercial competence.

Analytical Skills
We use this term in a broader sense than being able to analyze statistical data such as market information and financial reports, although these are undoubtedly important. The global account manager also needs to be able to make

sense of complex situations in order to develop account strategies and to evolve innovative value propositions and problem solutions for and with global customers. Appropriate modules that might be included in GAM development programs to meet these types of need are:

- *Strategy:* Developing an understanding of the strategy process as it relates to corporate business as well as global accounts with particular emphasis on the importance of the political aspects of strategy implementation.

- *Innovation, Entrepreneurship, and Problem Solving:* It might be argued that entrepreneurship is a personality trait rather than a learned skill. The entrepreneur, however, displays a number of behavioral attributes that can be learned: creativity, the ability to identify opportunity, and a facility to manage risk. For example, a core attribute of the entrepreneur is creativity, and courses should be designed to foster innovative ways of solving problems that can be applied to the global account management process.

- *GAM Implementation and Organizational Development:* GAM implementation involves the management of change and the selling of the value of GAM within as well as outside one's own organization. Global account managers need an understanding of the ways in which organizations function and how organizational design, systems, structures, and processes impact upon performance.

- *Quantitative Analysis:* Though the softer, more intuitive analytical skills are essential, so too are the skills of the quantitative analyst. The ability to analyze hard data and to apply statistical / analytical skills to problem resolution is a valuable asset to the global account manager.

Cultural Awareness

One of the dangers of increasing globalization is the concept of cultural colonialism. This occurs where the headquarters of the global corporation imposes their view of the world on subsidiary operations in other parts of the world. Culture has been defined as the way in which people solve the problems of living and interacting with each other. Different cultures have evolved different ways of resolving social issues, including the ways in which business is done. These different approaches have evolved in response to different cultural contexts because they work. To ignore these differences will result in unnecessary conflict and the erection of barriers to the GAM program. Global account managers' development programs must, for that reason, take account of cultural issues:

- *Foreign Languages:* While most international businesses conduct their affairs in English, many experienced senior managers of global account managers advocate that languages should be learned if for no other reason than that it breeds a degree of cultural understanding. It also projects a willingness, to foreign clients or the foreign subsidiary operations of global customers, to seek to understand them better through their language.

- *The Study of Culture:* The global account manager should be schooled in the differences in cultural perspective that exist between their home culture and the culture of the countries in which their customer operates. Even small "mistakes" can cause offense and produce barriers to doing business.

Business and Commercial Competence

The primary objective of GAM is to generate enhanced levels of profit from the global relationship. Any development program should therefore include modules that focus upon developing enhanced understanding about the international business environment:

- *International Industrial Marketing and Purchasing:* Underpinning the ability to formulate effective corporate and global account strategies must be a wider understanding of the way in which international industrial markets operate and the intricacies of modern purchasing processes. In addition, there is a need to understand operations management as it impacts upon the firm's ability to create global value propositions.

- *Marketing Channels:* Much of the global account manager's work is managed through internal and external intermediaries. Realizing the value of intermediaries as customers as well as channels to market is an important facet of global account manager's job.

- *Operations and Logistics Management:* The global promise can only be delivered if the supplier has successfully integrated their global operations and logistical processes. Global account managers require a detailed understanding of the operations of their own organization and how logistical capabilities can be leveraged to drive down costs and enhance value within the supply chain.

- *Information Technology:* A thorough knowledge of CRM, Marketing Information Systems, and account management software is necessary to facilitate communication between members of the GAM team and the customer.

- *Leadership and Team Management:* Learning to manage teams of people over whom you may have little line of authority and who are dispersed around the world is another core skill for global account managers. Understanding how teams work; what their component parts should be in order to make them effective; and how to coach, council, and motivate the people upon whom you depend to implement the global strategy are all skills that the global account manager as "team orchestrator" requires.

- *Communications:* Executive presentation skills, personal communication, social skills, and cross cultural communication capability are all important, as are writing skills.

- *International Finance:* A further requirement is for global account managers to be financially literate, able to read a balance sheet and manage budgets. An understanding of international finance is particularly important in order to facilitate the structuring of global agreements and the development of global pricing strategies.

This list of potential development programs is by no means exhaustive, but we feel that those mentioned here should form the backbone of training and development for global account managers and many members of their team.

The GAM Team

The nature of the GAM team has a major impact upon the ongoing success of the GAM program. Without team member support, it would be impossible for the global account manager alone to take care of all of the details necessary for success like gathering information, solving local problems, following up, and maintaining internal support. Besides the physical limitations imposed by the absence of an effective team, there are a number of additional factors that must be considered. These include how the team is structured, the clarity of reporting responsibilities, and the level of team involvement in the planning process, communication, and training. If any of these factors are left unresolved, the efficiency and effectiveness of the team, and thus the global account management program, will be greatly diminished.

The clarity of the reporting system can produce some problems if it is not in line with the goals of the GAM program. For example, if a GAM team member has a dual reporting role (that is, they report to both a global account manager and to a country director), the person has mixed loyalties. The problem is exacerbated when the team member is partially rewarded for their efforts and results by both the GAM program and the country manager. These dual-reporting systems tend only to work effectively where global/local issues have been resolved.

Ongoing Success

Ongoing success is dependent upon continued attention being paid to strategic, operational, and infrastructure issues. Success is firmly based upon successful teamwork embedded in a culture that prizes innovation, flexibility, and customer service.

Successful GAM programs build on success by maintaining effective communication that broadcasts the benefits of the program to both customers and colleagues. Internal education of colleagues to the benefits of GAM is an ongoing process aimed at sustaining internal buy-in. With continued executive support one of the main objectives is to institutionalize the process, refining organizational structures and molding the culture of the organization to align with the global strategic focus.

CHAPTER IX

Concluding Observations and Future Direction of GAM

CHAPTER IX: CONCLUDING OBSERVATIONS AND FUTURE DIRECTION OF GAM

Introduction

It became clear to us, during the research for this book, that while effective global account management may not be the exclusive preserve of large organizations, it is certainly the preserve of the sophisticated.

The GAM process is resource-hungry and makes heavy demands on finances and human resources. It demands the development of extraordinary capabilities in managing and coordinating operations, in managing people, and in creating value within the relationship between suppliers and their global customers. These capabilities, however, must be applied with subtlety and with complete understanding of the organizational complexity and cultural diversity that surrounds the process.

In writing this book, we do not claim to be offering the definitive guide to effective global account management. Our intention has been to share our observations of the GAM phenomenon, to stimulate debate in the area, and to afford our readers the opportunity to apply some of what we have learned within their own organizations. We hope that whatever stage of GAM development you have reached, whether you have had programs in place for a number of years or whether you are just beginning in your quest to find better ways to serve your global customers, that you will have found something of value between these pages.

What Have We Learned?

The following is a summary of some of the findings that have emerged from our studies, which we have explored in detail in the preceding chapters.

The Drivers
In many industries a number of common factors are driving the movement toward globalization and, consequently, the increasing use of global account management practices:

- Increasing demands from customers for higher degrees of operation coordination/integration with their suppliers, wherever they both operate in the world

- The impetus of changes in the economic environment: the emergence of global brands; increasing levels of industry concentration; the emergence of developing economies

- Rapidly changing technologies that facilitate process improvements, technological synergies, and communications

- The fundamental changes in the basis of competitive advantage, which has moved from being grounded in product capabilities to being dependent upon process and value-adding capabilities

Differentiate Between Global and Non-Global Customers
We have observed the reactions of companies to this process of globalization and recognized the importance of definition. Even if you use the term global as a generic term

that you apply to describe all your strategically important international customer relationships, it is important to differentiate between those that are truly global and those that are multi-national or regional in their operations. The difference between strategic accounts that operate in a truly global fashion and those that are, in reality, major international or regional players is the degree of strategic coordination they have achieved. You may perceive them to be of "global" significance to the future well being of your company, but do not try to treat them the same—you will fail. It is not possible to implement a global agreement with a non-global customer.

The Need for Supporting Systems and Processes
We have also become aware that the sales process is only a small part of the whole GAM program. In addition to being capable of interacting with the customer as a sales tool, the global account management team must be supported with a global product/service offering, with coordinated internal planning and reporting processes, information systems, equitable compensation programs, and a coordinated global operational capability supported by senior manager executive champions.

Supply Chain Capabilities
Global supply chain and channel management, as well as the integration of local sales and service provision with the global strategy, ensures that the global promise is delivered locally. It is through the development of strong logistical, process, and supply chain capabilities that opportunities for creating process efficiencies and economies can be identified and potential for adding value exploited.

The Global Account Manager

The skills and capabilities of the global account manager, the political entrepreneur, are crucial to the success of the program. These people are hard to find, and as interest in achieving global competitive advantage increases, they may become even more elusive. Although most existing global account managers are drawn from previous positions in sales and marketing, it may be wise for companies to seek to fill these posts with people drawn from other managerial and technical functions within the firm. This raises clear issues about training and development. It is our view that because of the need for detailed knowledge about the supplier's business, people, processes, systems, etc., the global account manager should, wherever possible, be promoted from within the firm rather than enlisted externally. If this is the case, firms should begin planning now for the development of people into the role.

Linked closely to the value of the global account manager role is the importance of senior manager executive sponsorship. Few programs were successful or enduring without the enthusiastic support and entanglement of champions drawn from the highest levels within the firm.

We are also aware that the demands of the global account management role are great and that there are inherent dangers in not consciously planning the career development paths of these valuable executives. There are two dangers in our view. The first is the danger of "burn-out" under the stress of constant travel, operating in different time zones, and managing in ambiguous and culturally diverse situations. The second relates to the danger of their changing employment and reflects the entrepreneurial nature of the people performing this role. An interesting, though purely anecdotal, observation is that several highly successful global account managers have left their jobs not in order to joint the "competition," but to engage in new business start-ups. This supports our view of global account managers as entrepreneurs but also gives a clear message to companies that if they wish to keep these people, they must recognize their need for constant challenge and plan their career development accordingly.

Organizing for Global Account Management

We have explored a number of ways in which companies organize the GAM effort. We are convinced that no one way is best (although there are certainly a number of generic tasks to be performed and positions filled) and that companies must reach decisions about structuring their GAM processes in ways that are contingent upon the needs of their customers and that achieve the maximum degree of coordination while considering existing arrangements and legacy structures. A pragmatic approach needs to be adopted that aims at developing a threshold level generic structure together with the flexibility to make adaptations to meet the needs of specific customers.

GAM Competencies

High levels of expertise are required of companies seeking to provide a global offering to their customers. These competencies are particularly evident in the areas of supply chain and logistics management, but also evident is the need to develop distinctive organizational, team, and personal competencies that add value to the GAM relationship. GAM competencies are revealed in the ability to manage the program, the global relationship, and the coordinating systems and processes.

Program Management must involve the support of a senior executive "champion" and should establish both the strategic vision and the organizational infrastructure that will

185

support the GAM process. Other elements of program management include the analysis of the company's customer base and the development of a portfolio of global accounts that facilitates account selection and the development of a generic global value proposition based upon the core competencies of the firm. In addition, program management includes the establishment of core support systems in terms of CRM and support functions within marketing and other specialist functional areas such as customer service, technical support, HRM, and IT.

Relationship Management involves client analysis and issue identification, as well the planning involved in developing the account's business potential. One of the major competencies in this process is the ability on the part of the global account manager and the account team to network effectively both within the client organization and their own in order to identify opportunity and the resources with which to exploit it.

Process Management involves the coordinating processes that link supplier with customer and includes the process by which the global value proposition is delivered at local level, the service process, and the internal back-up processes.

The Challenges
One of the major lessons from our studies is that GAM is difficult to implement and suffers from a number of major challenges. We have identified that these may be grouped into four categories: political; cultural; organizational; and practical encountered in both buyer and seller organizations, and emanating from the connecting systems, processes, and people.

The companies that have successfully met these challenges are those that have developed executive champions and sponsors of the program. They have recognized that those who oppose the program may have legitimate concerns and that it is equally important to sell the program in-house as it is to sell it to the customer. In addition, the global account manager and the GAM team make extensive use of communications and networking capabilities to promote the benefits of the program and to develop support.

Is GAM for Everyone?

For companies that lack the resources, geographical spread, or operational capability, GAM could prove a costly failure, but for those that aspire to being players on the international stage, despite some of the comments we make below, there is little alternative.

For smaller companies this poses a real problem, in that if they are unable to meet the needs of some of their most important customers in more than the national or regional arena, they are unlikely to retain their business. The answer here may be for them to develop capabilities in the area of strategic alliances and purposefully search for partners with whom they could evolve global collaborative value propositions.

There are certainly some industries, however, where even national strategic account management (SAM) seems to have been largely ignored; and there are individual companies that, while they have the potential to develop GAM programs, lack the will. These companies, some of which are large and powerful international organizations, have been successful in the past partly due to their disaggregated and divisionalized structures and the competitive advantage they have forged through product development and process capabilities.

Whether the few industries where we observed an absence of SAM initiatives will remain free from the effects of globalization and the need to develop GAM programs, we doubt; and to companies that steadfastly deny the need to configure their operations around customers, we suggest that they think again. In all industries that we observed, the foundations of competitive advantage were moving from product/technical capability, toward some manifestation of enhanced customer service. It is our belief that those companies that do not recognize the drives to change will have difficulty surviving, in their present form, into the future.

The Future?

While increasing numbers of companies are adopting GAM as a management process, certainly those headquartered in Europe and North America, there are still a surprising number of substantial companies that do not even practice national strategic account management. This raises the question, is GAM merely the latest management fad, or does it have a long-term future?

In our view, while it may take different forms depending upon the cultural perspective adopted by the parent organization, and despite short-term fluctuations in economic activity, the phenomenon of global buyer-supplier collaboration will increase in most industries.

How effective companies become at managing the global interface with their customers will depend to some extent upon their ability to reconcile the ambiguity inherent in thinking globally **and** locally—and acting appropriately.

The adversity that companies face in managing their global operations against a background of existing "heritage" structures, systems, and processes means that the GAM program must strive to be inherently flexible, and our observations would suggest that in the future companies will be increasingly willing to experiment in the way they do business together.

What this means in practice is that we may well be witnessing the emergence of new forms of economic organization, whereby the traditional boundaries between buyers and sellers blur. Where collaboration between members of the supply chain extends to collaborative sourcing and outsourcing, co-product development, integrated operations management and marketing, it may be increasingly difficult to determine where one organization ends and the next begins, except to those closely involved in the process. Where elements of one organization join teams from other organizations, in effect what emerges is a third, *virtual* organization. This may exist only for the duration of a specific project and continually reform as new projects are identified. A further development may, however, be the emergence of semi-permanent virtual organizations that absorb and reconfigure the core competencies of the parent companies into quasi-independent businesses. Controlling these multiple virtual organizations may become the major focus for international managerial attention. Where this happens the new skills that will be demanded of international managers will be very close to those we have observed in the very best global account managers, those we have labeled *political entrepreneurs*.

In the role of political entrepreneur, we see emerging a new functional area of management. This role goes beyond that of managing relationships to providing the link between the strategic hearts of buyer-seller organizations. It is a role that is essentially concerned with the realization of synergistic entrepreneurial value, with managing the coordination of virtual organizations, and with creating new *businesses*, rather than just new business. When this role is considered together with the emergence of the new forms of economic organization, skills and competencies that are demanded of the people who fill this role, coupled with the experience they gain through performing it, suggests that it is from their ranks that the next generation of senior executives within major international companies will be drawn.

The GAM phenomenon is most evident in Europe and North America. There is some question in our minds whether, in its Western form, GAM will easily transfer to

---

That this process (globalization) is already underway is seldom a contentious issue. Much of the debate focuses on the speed of globalization, the stage reached in different parts of the world, how much is desirable, and the context to which decisions taken in one part of the world affect another. For multi-national selling companies operating in business-to-business markets it is about global strategic direction and responding to globally dispersed customers. This leads inevitably to the question, "How global and how local should our approach be in particular industries?" Clearly, competing and operating in the food industry is not the same as in chemicals, motor vehicles, financial services, defense, etc.

Tony Millman
"How Well Does the Concept of Global Account Management Travel Across Cultures?"
The Journal of Selling and Major Account Management. Vol.2, No.2 (Winter, 2000).
The Sales Research Trust Ltd., Southampton, U.K.

---

other parts of the world. Two fundamental characteristics of GAM are that it provides a single point of contact for customers and that its implementation is heavily dependent upon effective teamwork. In the West, account managers are normally given the power to make independent decisions (within agreed guidelines) in relation to their accounts. This may not be the case in other high-context, collective cultures that rely more heavily upon consensus management. The value of a single point of contact becomes dissipated when there is a need for continual consultation with other members of the selling organization.

Over the issue of teamwork, there is also some uncertainty. While strong anecdotal evidence suggests that Japanese teams work well at the level of the national account, less is known about their response to working within

---

Research conducted by the authors in the U.S. and Europe has revealed many references to 'national barons'—positions reinforced by performance measures related to the boundaries of business units and countries. Less is known about the nature of such fiefdoms in Asia, but the mind boggles at the thought of rolling out a global account program encompassing, say, China. At national level, China's brand of Communism and bureaucracy adheres to central planning, though somewhat relaxed in recent years. At local level, guanxi networks pervade the business culture, which are built around personalized hierarchies and highly localized feudalism. One-point-three billion people—what chance Western-style GAM? The 'travelability' of the GAM concept is largely dependent upon how well its originators understand their own and host business cultures, the extent to which systems/processes require local adaptation, and the quality of the 'human bridge' provided by people involved in managing the transfer process.'

Tony Millman

---

a multi-cultural environment, and some writers urge caution in trying to apply the Euro-American, systems-oriented approach in more collectivist cultures.

Other problems become apparent when issues of incentives, negotiation styles, and gender are considered. In addition, while problems have been encountered because of the threat globalization poses to the scope of their jobs and the decision-making autonomy of general country and national account managers within a largely European and North American cultural context, these problems may be even more difficult to manage in other cultural and economic contexts.

As the developing economies of the world mature, the challenges associated with integrating them into the global economy will increase, but so, too, will the potential for finding creative new ways of doing business around the world. We end this book with a quotation we used at its beginning, but warn against the supposition that the models for GAM that have been developed in North America and in Europe will be effective wherever they are applied. We have observed the emergence of GAM processes and we are sure of only of one thing, that these processes are still emerging and that those companies that aspire to being and remaining global players must be flexible, open minded, innovative, and tolerant of ambiguity and cultural diversity.

> The question for all companies, in all industries and all around the world, is not *whether* to go global. The question is *when?* The truth is that as your customers increasingly globalize their operations, you must be able to serve them consistently wherever they operate in the world, or you will soon cease to serve them *anywhere* in the world.

APPENDIX

ABOUT THE AUTHORS

Dr. Kevin Wilson is the CEO of the Sales Research Trust Ltd., author of numerous articles on selling and strategic account management and contributor to a number of books. Kevin's research and consultancy interests lie in the areas of international marketing, sales management, and strategic global account management. He is an international speaker and recognized expert in the field of GAM.

Professor Tony Millman, from the University of Buckingham School of Business, is a leading researcher in the field of strategic account management. Author of numerous research papers, articles, and a contributor to several books, Tony's industrial experience is drawn from the aerospace and plastics industries. His current research interests lie in international business and global account management.

Dr. Dan Weilbaker is Standard Register Professor of Sales at Northern Illinois University and a visiting professor at the Southampton Business School, U.K. Dan has published in a wide range of academic journals and was a contributor to a previous SAMA publication, *Unlocking Profits*. He is a member of the editorial review boards of the *Journal of Selling and Major Account Management*, the *Journal of Personal Selling and Sales Management*, the *Journal of Marketing Education*, and the *Marketing Education Review*, and has undertaken consultancy work for a wide range of companies including Motorola, Sandoz Corporation, Schering Plough Corporation, and Eli Lilly and Company. Dan serves on the Board of

Directors of the Professional Society for Sales and Marketing Training. He has been a member of the Strategic Account Management Association for five years and was on the Board of Directors of SAMA for three years.

Dr. Simon R Croom., BA, MSc Ph.D., FCIPS, FRSA

Dr Simon Croom is a Lecturer in Operations Management at Warwick Business School. Simon's primary area of expertise is e-business in the supply chain, and he has recently completed a major study of e-business developments in supply chains. He has published fifty technical papers in the areas of e-business, supply chain management, strategic procurement, and global account management. Prior to joining Warwick Business School, Simon was Assistant Director of the Manufacturing and Supply Chain Management Centre at Coventry University. Simon's industrial experience includes six years purchasing and supply chain management in the engineering and auto industries, and ten years as owner-director of a retail organization. He is an advisor on procurement to the United Kingdom's Office of Government Commerce, and in recent years Simon has acted for a number of major global corporations as an advisor on supply chain management and e-business strategy. Simon is a Director of the Sales Research Trust.

ABOUT THE SPONSORS

The Strategic Account Management Association

SAMA Mission Statement

The Strategic Account Management Association is a non-profit organization devoted to developing and promoting the concept of customer-supplier partnering. SAMA is dedicated to the professional and personal development of the executives charged with managing national, global and strategic account relationships, and to elevating the status of the profession as a whole.

A Brief History

- SAMA was founded in 1964 by E. Brooke Lee and a group of sales executives in the chemical industry to respond to a need for training on the specifics of managing large, complex, multi-location accounts.

- SAMA services and values apply to all industries. Among our membership are companies in: communications, hospitality, manufacturing, chemicals, electronics, food, paper, health care, textiles, services, utilities, and many other manufacturing segments.

- Today, over 2000 members strong, SAMA remains unique in its focus on assisting its members in building and managing successful partnerships with their core accounts.

SAMA Benefits & Services

SAMA is the Strategic Account Management profession's leading source of comprehensive trend and research information. The association provides its members with the training, knowledge, and networking opportunities required to successfully manage Strategic Account programs:

Conferences / Seminars

SAMA's conferences and seminars provide Strategic Account Management professionals with unique and valuable Strategic Account Management training opportunities.

The Annual Conference, held each May, is the association's signature event, bringing together over 1,200 SAMs to share best practices, learn new tools and network with peers. European Conferences are customized to meet the unique needs of Strategic / Global Account Management professionals working in the diverse European cultural environment. SAMA University offers skill-building workshops in an interactive learning environment, taught by some of the best trainers and consultants in the world. They will deliver practical information and provide tools that you can use immediately to improve your program as well as your personal skills. The Annual Executive Leadership Symposium is designed to provide a unique forum for leaders of Strategic Account programs to discuss common issues, share experiences, debate controversial problems and develop capabilities to improve their own effectiveness. This event is restricted to genuine peers - executives with general management responsibility for key customer initiatives and overall corporate strategy.

Knowledge Resources

To provide members with the high quality and cutting-edge information they need, the SAMA Education & Information department is constantly scanning the global SAM landscape and making findings available to members. The association's on-line Digital Library is available 24 hours a day, containing all past issues of *Velocity*™, Research Briefs, Best Practices, Case Studies, and much more.

Networking Opportunities

SAMA understands the importance of building a strong peer network to share ideas, challenges and solutions. All educational events therefore provide attendees with many networking opportunities. In addition, the e-mail based Special Interest Groups (SIGs) encourage open discussion in a convenient yet effective electronic environment, and the on-line Peer Network allows members to contact colleagues who are experts in one of a vast array of topics.

> SAMA provides the ideal environment to exchange thoughts with strategic account management peers. Why repeat the same failures over and over? Increase your SAM program's success by taking advantage of SAMA's wealth of information on the newest trends and changes in the strategic account management profession.
>
> Hermann Weiffenbach
> VP & Director, Deutsche Telekom Account, Motorola

The Sales Research Trust

The Sales Research Trust Ltd (SRT) is a not-for-profit organization providing a focus for collaboration between practitioners and academics for the advancement of education and research in the areas of selling and strategic customer account management.

The SRT began as a loose association of academics intent upon running a symposium, The First International Symposium on Selling and Major Account Management, in 1997. Since then, it has grown into a vast network of practitioners and academics spanning Europe and North America, with contacts in Australia, Japan, and Singapore.

The SRT has a board of directors and an advisory board drawn from leading academic institutions within the United Kingdom. We have a number of close relationships with researchers in France, Switzerland, Ireland, the United States, and the United Kingdom. We also work closely with the Strategic Account Management Association of Chicago, IL, the Sales Institute of Ireland, and a number of leading edge consultancy organizations.

The primary aim of the SRT is to promote *Better Practice through Research*.